KHANIQAHI NIMATULLAHI
(SUFI ORDER)

306 West 11th Street
New York, NY, 10014 -USA
Tel: 212 924.7739
Fax: 212 924.5479

4931 MacArthur Blvd. NW
Washington, DC 20007 -USA
Tel: 202-338.4757

84 Pembroke Street
Boston, MA 02118 -USA
Tel: 617-536.0076

4642 North Hermitage
Chicago, IL 60640 -USA
Tel: 312-561.1616

4021 19th Avenue
San Francisco, CA 94132 -USA
Tel: 415-586.1313

11019 Arleta Avenue
Mission Hills,
Los Angeles, CA 91345 -USA
Tel: 818-365.2226

219 Chace Street
Santa Cruz, CA 95060 -USA
Tel: 408-425.8454

405 Greg Avenue
Santa Fe, NM 87501 -USA
Tel: 505-983.8500

310 NE 57th Street
Seattle, WA 98105 -USA
Tel: 206-527.5018

41 Chepstow Place
London W2 4TS
England
Tel: 071-229-0769

The Old Windmill, Sulgrave,
Banbury, Oxfordshire
OX17 2SH England
Tel: 0295-760.361

95 Old Lansdowne Rd.
West Disdbury, Manchester,
M20 8NZ, England
Tel: 061-434.8857

Kölnerstraße 176
5000 Köln 90 (Porz)
Germany
Tel: 49-2203.15390

Van Blankenburgstraat 66B
2517 XS 's-Gravenhage,
The Netherlands
Tel: 070-345.0251

50 Rue du 4ème Zouaves
Rosny-sous-Bois 93110,
Paris, France
Tel: 48-552.809

Viale Liberazione, 1
Vaiano Cremasco (CR)
Milan, Italy
Tel: 39-373.277.246

63 Boulevard Latrille
BP 1224 Abidjan
CIDEX 1 Côte d'Ivoire
Africa
Tel: 225-410.510

87A Mullen Street
Balmain, 2041
Sydney, Australia
Tel: 612-555.7546

SUFISM I

NIMATULLAHI SUFI ORDER
656 EMILY DRIVE
MT. VIEW, CA 94043
(650) 960 - 3429

KHANIQAHI NIMATULLAHI
(SUFI ORDER)

Also available by Dr. Javad Nurbakhsh

SUFISM I

Meaning, Knowledge, and Unity

Dr. Javad Nurbakhsh

KHANIQAHI-NIMATULLAHI PUBLICATIONS
LONDON & NEW YORK

Book design by Shari DeMiskey
Cover design by Alex Cowie

Library of Congress Catalog Card Number 81-81725

ISBN 09-933546-05-X
Second printing 1993

Printed in the United States of America on Acid Free Paper

Published by Khaniqahi-Nimatullahi Publications (KNP)
306 West 11th Street
New York, New York 10014 USA
Telephone: (212) 924-7739
Facsimile: (212) 924-5479

Contents

TASAVVOF

Definitions of Sufism and the Sufi

THE DERIVATION OF THE WORD "SUFI"

MANY different opinions and interpretations have been offered concerning the derivation of the word *sufi*. Of these, two deserve particular attention, the second of which is in fact more accurate.

1. Abu Rayhān Biruni derived the word *sufi* from the Greek *sophia,* meaning wisdom, which also forms the root of the word "philosophy" *(philo + sophia,* "the love of wisdom"). Biruni maintained that Moslems who held views similar to those of the Greek sages were given this name.

2. The best-known (and more accurate) opinion on the origin of the word is that it comes from *suf,* meaning "wool," and signifies "pertaining to wool," the term being used because Sufis wore woolen robes. From ancient times it was the custom of ascetics, the poor, and the pious to wear such garments.

As the Prophet of Islam said, "You should wear garments of wool that you may find in your hearts the sweetness of faith." *(Kashf al-mahjub)*

Shehāb ad-Din Sohravardi, in his classic of Sufism, the *'Avāref al-ma'āref,* cites the following tradition, attributed to Anas ebn Mālek, "The Messenger of God would accept invitations even from slaves, ride upon donkeys, and wear (coarse) woolen clothes." Moreover, both Jesus and Moses, according to legend, also used to wear wool.

Hasan of Basra has related that he met seventy of the Prophet's Companions, veterans of the Battle of Badr, and that all of them wore wool. Jalāl al-Din Rumi also considered wool the appropriate dress for Sufis.

In short, the Sufis chose to wear wool to indicate their rejection of the luxuries of the world and to demonstrate to those who desired to enter the Spiritual Path that Sufism demanded ascetic practices.

EARLY EXAMPLES OF THE USE OF THE WORD "SUFI"

In his *Kitāb al-loma',* Abu Nasr Sarraj states:

In a book devoted to the history of Mecca, Mohammad ebn Eshāq relates, "Before the advent of Islam, when no one was circumambulating the *ka'aba,* a man who was a Sufi arrived one day from a distant city. He entered the Sacred Precinct, made the circumambulation, and then went his way again."

Sarrāj also quotes Hasan of Basra as saying, "I once saw a Sufi circumambulating the *ka'aba.* I tried to give him something, but he refused, saying, 'I have two thirds of a silver dirham, and that will suffice me.'"

Again Sarrāj relates that the Sufi Sofyān Thawri (d. 161/778) said, "If it were not for Abu Hāshem, the Sufi, I would never have realized how subtle my own hypocrisy can be." By this evidence, and a comparison of dates, it would appear that this Abu Hāshem was the first person in Islam to be called a Sufi.

Perhaps most appropriate of all, however, are these lines of Abol-Fath al-Bosti:

> *People quarrel about the word "sufi,"*
> *From ancient times deriving it from "wool,"*
> *But I ascribe the name to a chivalrous youth*
> *Who loving God sincerely* (sāfā)
> *And being loved sincerely* (sufi) *by Him*
> *Thus deserved the title "Sufi."*

SHADES OF MEANING BETWEEN *SUFI, DARVISH, ZĀHED,* AND *FAQIR*

The Persian word *darvish,* or "dervish" in English, means "poor person" or "pauper." Since most Sufis renounced worldly possessions, they were known by this term—although a Sufi need not be "poor," nor is every "poor one" a Sufi.

As for the Arabic word *zāhed,* if it be considered in its literal sense of an "ascetic" or one who has renounced the world, then indeed most Sufis, especially in early Islam, were zāheds. However, many Sufis have taken the word to describe one who renounces this world for the sake of reward in the next; and if this is so, then *sufi* and *zāhed* cannot mean the same thing. Sufis renounce the world out of love for God, not hope of reward. Bāyazid Bastāmi said, "My period of asceticism lasted but three days: on the first

I renounced the world, on the second I renounced the
world to come, and on the third I renounced everything
but God."

The people of Damascus used the terms *sufi* and *faqir*
(meaning "poor one," like *darvish*) interchangeably, for
they believed that God, in the *Koran,* was referring to Sufis
when He mentioned, "the poor, those who are constrained
in the way of God" (II: 273).

One must realize, however, that there are two types of
poverty, one merely formal or external, the other genuine.

Formal poverty itself can be of two kinds. The first is
the involuntary poverty of one who lacks possessions but
desires them; such a person may be called a beggar and
has no special virtue. The second is the voluntary poverty
of one who renounces the world of his own volition. This,
however, is not a characteristic of Sufism, since the Sufi
concerns himself with God's will, rather than with his own,
in relation to external things. He sees virtue in neither outward and formal poverty nor in outward and formal
wealth, but only in that which accords with God's will. The
one who is "voluntarily poor" seeks recompense in heaven
for his renunciation of this world; the Sufi, however, renounces all, not to earn a promised reward but simply out
of love for his Lord. He is "the son of the present moment," and in this eternal present turns his attention
toward God alone. As Abu 'Abdollāh Khafif put it, "The
Sufi is chosen by God Himself to love Him; the faqir purifies himself in poverty that he might gain nearness to
God."

True or genuine poverty, however, is identical with
what may be called Sufism, and when a Sufi is called a
faqir, it is generally in this sense of the word. Thus the
Prophet of God has said:

The *Shari'at* (God's Law) is my words, the *Tariqat*
(Spiritual Path) is my acts, and *Haqiqat* ("Truth,"

God Himself) is my inward state. Knowledge is the chief of my possessions, intelligence is my religion, love my foundation, intense yearning my steed, fear my friend, science my weapon, forbearance my companion, trust my cloak, contentment my treasure, truthfulness my station, certainty my refuge, and poverty my pride. I am prouder of it than all the other attributes of God's prophets. *(al-Mojli)*

True poverty is detachment from all possessions; the Prophet's pride was in this, not in any form of formal or outward poverty. Many were the poor of Mecca, but they were not detached.

"Detachment from all possessions" means, for the faqir, that he considers nothing his own, so much so that he is dead to his own self. Sufis say, "the faqir needs nothing and nothing needs him"; this is the spiritual station of pure and utter Oneness *(vahdat-e serf)*, the unadulterated profession of Divine Unity *(tawhid-e mahd)*. That is, when one ceases to attribute things to oneself, one realizes God's Unity, which is why the Sufis say, "The profession of Unity *(Tawhid)* is to nullify all attributions."

Asked to define "faqir," Hallāj answered, "He is one who is independent of all but God, who gazes only upon Him." *(Tadhkerat al-awliyā')* In a similar vein, Shebli remarked, "The faqir's wealth and independence are only in God." *(Kashf al-mahjub)*

Again, it is said that "when poverty *(faqr)* is perfected, there is only God." According to the Prophet, "Poverty is blackness of face in the two worlds." *(al-Mojli)* The Sufis interpret "blackness" in this sense as the annihilation of the wayfarer in both this world and the next, for blackness is darkness, and "darkness" *(zolmah)* in Arabic often symbolizes nonexistence and annihilation.

The Prophet also said, "Poverty can reach the point of

infidelity *(kofr)." (al-Mojli)* Paradoxical as it may seem, the Prophet is in fact referring to true poverty here. When the true faqir reaches the station of detachment from all possessions, he ceases to attribute anything to himself; nothing remains for him but the Being of the One Essence, the Being of God. It was in such a station that the "shocking" sayings of Bayāzid were made, such as "Glory be to me! How exalted is my station!" and "Nothing lies beneath my cloak but God!", as well as Hallāj's proclamation, "I am the Truth." From the exoteric point of view of the *Shari'at,* such assertions are blasphemy and unbelief, but in the language of the *Tariqat* and *Haqiqat,* they are the simple truth.

DEFINITIONS OF "SUFISM" AND "SUFI"

Sufi masters have offered numerous and seemingly varied definitions of Sufism and the Sufi. These differences, however, arose only from the fact that each master was speaking from his own spiritual station to the station and level of understanding of his listeners. Thus, each definition uncovers a different aspect of Sufism, each correct in its proper context, and to grasp Sufism as a whole, one must consider as wide a range of definitions as possible. In order to clarify the nature of Sufism, therefore, the following definitions have been chosen and assembled, definitions that through study will lead to a more profound understanding of the two terms.

SAYINGS OF THE MASTERS ON SUFISM *(TASAVVOF)*

1. Jonayd, asked to define Sufism, replied, "It is that one

should be with God, without any attachment (to other than Him)." *(al-Loma')*

2. Hojviri has quoted Jonayd as also saying, "Sufism is based on eight qualities: generosity, contentment, patience, allusion, exile, the wearing of wool, travel and poverty. Generosity is symbolized by Abraham, contentment by Isaac, patience by Job, allusion by Zacharias, exile by John, the wearing of wool by Moses, travel by Jesus, and poverty by Mohammad. God bless them all and give them peace!"

Hojviri comments:

> Sufism is founded upon eight qualities, amounting to the emulation of eight different prophets. Generosity pertains to Abraham, who would have sacrificed his own son; contentment to Isaac, happy with God's command, who bade farewell to his own precious life; patience to Job, uncomplaining of his loathsome sores; allusion to Zacharias, who God says "called upon his Lord secretly" (Koran XIX, 3); exile to John, outcast from his own land, a stranger among his own people; travel to Jesus, so detached in his wandering that he owned no more than comb and cup (yet when he saw someone drinking from cupped hands, threw away his cup, and when he saw another combing his hair with his fingers, threw away his comb). As for Moses, all his garments were of wool; and as for Mohammad, he himself said, "Poverty is my pride." *(Kashf al-mahjub)*

3. Jonayd further said: "Sufism is that God makes you die to yourself and live in Him." *(Resālat al-Qoshayri)*

4. And again, "Sufism is toil without respite" (or "war [against the ego] with no peace"). *(Ibid)*

5. And again, "Sufism is remembrance *(dhekr)* in a gathering, ecstasy in hearing, and practice by emulation." *(Ibid)* That is, remembrance in an assembly aids the individual Sufi in turning his attention towards God; "ecstasy in hearing" refers to the heart's apprehension of the roots of those divine inspirations contained within acts of worship, as well as to the manner in which man's innermost consciousness (his *serr* or "secret") listens to those subtle allusions that guide him towards contemplation and encounter with the Divine; and "practice by emulation" means the inward and outward imitation of the Prophet himself.

6. Jonayd has also said, "Sufism is election; the Sufi is chosen (by God) from amongst all those things that are 'other-than-Him.' " *(Ibid)*

7. And again:

> *The science of Sufism is a science unknown*
> *But to the Brothers of wisdom, whom only God knows.*
> *It is known to no one who has not witnessed it,*
> *For how can a blind man see the light of the sun?*

8. On another occasion, when asked about Sufism, Jonayd responded, "It is the purification of the heart from all conformity with creatures, the separation of oneself from the moral attitudes of the natural world, and the stamping out of all the attributes of human nature. It is to shun everything to which the ego *(nafs)* beckons you, to keep company with the qualities of spiritual men, to hold fast to the sciences of the Truth, to be always busy with what is appropriate (to a Sufi), to give sincere admonition to all Moslems, to keep faith with God, and to follow the Prophet in the *Shari'at*." *(Asrār al-tawhid)*

9. Jonayd also said, "Sufism is a quality; the servant takes up residence within it."

He was then asked, "A quality of God or of the individual?"

"In essence," he replied, "a quality of God, but outwardly of the Sufi himself. That is, its being demands the annihilation *(fanā')* of the servant's attributes, which in turn implies the subsistence *(baqā')* of God's Attributes. So Sufism is a quality of God, even though outwardly it demands constant striving on the Sufi's part, which is an attribute of the servant." *(Kashf al-Mahjub)*

10. Asked about the essence of Sufism, Jonayd replied, "You must accept its outward aspect and ask nothing of its essence, for that would be to commit an injustice against it." *(Tadhkerat al-awliyā')*

11. He also said, "Sufism is remembrance, then ecstasy, then neither one nor the other, lest it be thought to be something it is not!" *(Ibid)*

12. And again, "Sufism is to regard the moments. The Sufi should not gaze beyond his limits, nor face any but his Lord, nor concern himself with anything but his own 'moment.' " *(Kholāse-ye sharh-e ta'arrof)*

13. Abu Sa'id Abel-Khayr, when asked, "What is Sufism?", replied, "What's in your head—toss it away! What's in your hand—give it up! Whatever happens—don't turn away from it." *(Asrār al-tawhid)*

14. On another occasion, in response to the same question, Abu Sa'id answered, "Sufism is patience before God's commands and prohibitions, contentment and submission to destiny's course." Then he added, "A high and noble state will never overtake you unless it is rooted in patience,

contentment, and submission to God's predestination and decrees." *(Ibid.)*

15. Once, at a Sufi meeting, Abu Sa'id declared, "This is Sufism: high rank in disgrace, wealth in poverty, Lordship in service, satiety in hunger, attire in nakedness, freedom in slavery, life in death, sweetness in bitterness. Whosoever enters upon this path but makes no progress in these matters will become daily more lost!" *(Ibid)*

16. Another time, Abu Sa'id said, "Sufism is God's will for His creatures, without the creatures." He explained, "Change, inconstancy, agitation and bother all rise from the ego *(nafs)*. Let one glimmer of Truth's lights be unveiled, however, and all noise and tumult, all change and variegation, vanish. With God is no depression, with the ego no comfort." *(Ibid)*

17. And again, "Academic Sufism is like a house built on excrement!" He went on to add, "This thing (true Sufism) cannot be stitched on with needle and thread, nor tied on with twine. It cannot be completed with words. Blood does not flow without an incision; Sufism only reaches its end through humble supplication. One must be in need." *(Ibid)*

18. He also said, "First Sufism was pain; only later did it become something to write about!" *(Ibid)*

19. On another occasion, in reply to the question, "What is Sufism?", Abu Sa'id answered, "Idolatry!"

"But why, O Shaykh?" he was asked.

"Sufism," he explained, "is to separate the heart from all 'others' and all 'parts.' But there is no 'other,' no 'part!' "

20. Abu Sa'id once quoted Mohammad ebn 'Ali al-

Aqssāb, who said, "Sufism was first a spiritual state; then it became words; then both state and words vanished, and charlatanism took their place." *(Ibid)*

21. "One day Abu Sa'id and some disciples passed by a water mill. The Shaykh reined in his horse and sat staring at the mill for some time. 'Do you hear what this mill is saying?' he asked the others. 'It says, "Sufism is that which I do: I take the coarse and return it as fine; I turn ceaselessly about myself, making a journey within myself, that I might put away from myself everything that does not belong there." ' "*(Ibid)*

22. Abu Sa'id also said, "Sufism is but a name; when it is finished, only God remains." *(Ibid)*

23. He also said, "Seven hundred Sufi masters have spoken of the Path, and the last said the same as the first. Their words were different perhaps, but their intention was one. Sufism is the abandonment of affectation. And of all your affectations none is weightier than your "you-ness." When you are occupied with yourself, you remain far from Him." *(Ibid)*

24. And again, "Seven hundred masters have discoursed upon Sufism, but the best and most concise of their sayings is this: Sufism is to seize the moment and use it appropriately." *(Ibid)*

25. And again, "Sufism consists of two things: looking in one direction and living in one way." *(Ibid)*

26. And finally, "Sufism is the heart standing with God, with nothing in between." *(Ibid)*

27. Abu 'Ali Rudbāri has said, "Sufism is the gift of God's

free men." *(Tadhkerat al-awliyā')*

28. Rudbāri also said, "Sufism is to weep at the Beloved's door, even if He spurns you." *(Resālat al-Qoshayri)*

29. And again, "It is the clarity of proximity after the obscurity of separation." *(Ibid)*

30. According to Abol-Qāsen Nasrābādi, "Sufism is to adhere to and act by the *Koran* and the example of the Prophet, abandoning self-will and innovation, honoring and respecting the masters, regarding both the esteem and anger of others as nothing; it is the regular recitation of the litanies and the avoidance of all liberal interpretations (of the *Koran* and tradition)." *(Rasā'el-e Khwājeh 'Abdollāh Ansāri)*

31. Abu Sa'id A'rābi: "Sufism—all of it—is to abandon excess." *(Nafahāt al-ons)*

32. Abu Na'im Esfahāni: "Sufism is to guard against slips and awake from laziness." *(Helyat al-awliyā')*

33. Abu Na'im: "Sufism is to maintain loving sincerity and to abandon perfidy" *(Ibid)*

34. Abu Na'im: "Sufism is to liberate oneself from the transitory and what is passing and to take pleasure in what is abiding and permanent." *(Ibid)*

35. Abu Na'im: "Sufism is to acknowledge one's debt to God and to conceal one's afflictions." *(Ibid)*

36. Abu Na'im: "Sufism is to adhere to humility and happiness, to root up restlessness and impatience." *(Ibid)*

37. Abu Na'im: "Sufism is devotion to degradations and duties, a preference for smallnesses and anonymities." *(Ibid)*

38. Abu Na'im: "Sufism is contentment with one's portion and generosity with one's bounty." *(Ibid)*

39. Abu Na'im: "Sufism is wakefulness, attentiveness, and discernment in fending off all fantasy and nonsense." *(Ibid)*

40. Abu Na'im: "Sufism is holding fast to reverence and persevering in service." *(Ibid)*

41. Abu Na'im: "Sufism is to seize the moment and hold to the Way." *(Ibid)*

42. Abu Na'im: "Sufism is generosity in giving and patience in persecution." *(Ibid)*

43. Abu Na'im: "Sufism is to seize the opportunity for remembrance and to conceal the secret." *(Ibid)*

44. Khwājeh 'Abdollāh Ansāri: "A Sufi is a handful of dust, passed through a sieve, then moistened with a few drops of water. Trodden upon, it neither bruises nor muddies the foot of the passerby." *(Rasā'el-e Ansāri)*

45. Ansāri: "What is Sufism? Outwardly colorless, inwardly at peace." *(Ibid)*

46. Sari Saqati: "Sufism is a word that signifies three characteristics: the Sufi's light of gnosis never extinguishes the candle of his piety; he does not speak of esoteric knowledge which contradicts the exoteric meaning of the *Koran* and traditions; and he never allows his own miraculous

deeds to unveil the secrets of saints or sinners." *(Tadhkerat al-awliyā')*

Ansāri has rendered these words into Persian and commented on them in the following way:

> Sufism has three meanings. First, the light of gnosis does not extinguish the light of piety, but rather increases it; that is, the Sufi's knowledge of God never lessens the light of his fear of God. Second, he does not speak of an esoteric knowledge, the outward expression of which would offend against God's Book and the sacred Shari'at of His Messenger. Third, his miracles never inspire him to lift a single veil from the secrets of God's servants. *(Rasā'el-e Ansāri)*

47. Ma'ruf Karkhi: "Sufism is to grasp the realities, speak of the subtleties, and despair of everything else in creation." *(Tadhkerat al-awliyā)*

48. Abu 'Othmān Maghrebi: "Sufism is the severance of attachments, the rejection of creatures, and union with the realities." *(Ibid)*

49. Abu Bakr Shebli: "Sufism is to sit without cares with God." *(Resalāt al-Qoshayri)*

50. Shebli: "Sufism is an all-consuming flash of lightning." *(Ibid)*

51. Shebli: "Sufism is to be protected from gazing upon created existence." *(Ibid)*

52. Shebli: "Sufism is to be as you were before you came to be." *(Tadhkerat al-awliyā')*

53. Shebli: "Sufism is to control the faculties and observe the breaths." *(Ibid)*

54. Shebli: "Sufism is idolatry. It prevents the heart from gazing upon 'other,' but no 'other' exists! In other words, if one affirms God's Unity, then to see anything other than God is idolatry *(sherk)*. But the 'other' has no value in the heart; to preserve the heart from remembering the 'other'— how absurd!" *(Kashf al-mahjub)*

55. Abol-Hasan Bushanji: "Sufism is minimal hope and unceasing perseverance." *(Tadhkerat al-awliyā')*

56. Bushanji: "Today Sufism is a name without a reality, whereas it was once a reality without a name!" *(Kashf al-mahjub)*

57. Ja'far Kholdi: "Sufism is to throw the ego *(nafs)* into slavery, emerge from human nature, and gaze wholly upon God." *(Tadhkerat al-awliyā')*

58. Kholdi: "In Sufism, the essence of Lordship unfolds while the essence of slavehood fades away." *(Ibid)*

59. Abu Eshāq ebn Ebrāhim once saw the Prophet in a dream and asked him about Sufism. The Prophet replied, "It is to abandon all claims and conceal all meanings." *(Nafahāt al-ons;* in the *Tadhkerat al-awliyā',* the saying is attributed to Kholdi).

60. Abol-Hasan Sirvāni: "Sufism is one-pointed concentration and solitude (with God)." *(Tarā'eq al-haqā'eq)*

61. Sirvani: "Sufism is to abandon creation and to make one's spiritual resolve one-pointed." *(Ibid)*

62. Abol-Hassan Hosri: "Sufism is the purification of the heart from the turbidity of oppositions." *(Tadhkerāt al-awliyā')*

63. The Caliph asked Hosri about Sufism, and he replied, "It is to find no rest in earth or heaven without Him."

The Caliph asked, "Then what?"

He answered, "You turn over your affairs to Him, for He is God, and by His decree you will be made nothing."

Again the Caliph asked, "Then?"

Hosri replied, "What is there after the truth save error *(Koran,* X: 32)? When one finds the Truth, one does not look back to something else!" *(Tadhkerāt al-awliyā')*

64. Abol-'Abbās Nahāvandi: "Sufism is to conceal one's spiritual state and relinquish all honor to one's spiritual brethren." *(Ibid)*

65. Abol-Hosayn Nuri: "Sufism is neither formal practice nor science, but rather moral qualities and virtues." The author of the *Kashf al-mahjub* comments, "If Sufism were formal practice, it could be acquired through effort; if it were science, it could be learned through study. But Sufism is virtues; seek within yourself for their properties and apply them correctly within yourself; pay from yourself their just price, or you will never acquire Sufism.

"The difference between formal practice and virtue is that the former is an activity inspired by personal motives and affectations such that the inner and the outer man are in conflict; such action lacks spiritual significance. Virtues are also actions, but praise-worthy, devoid of all affectation and dubious motives. The outward harmonizes with the inward; all pretension vanishes."

66. Nuri: "Sufism is liberation, chivalry, the giving up of affectation, and generosity. Liberation is to be free of self

will; chivalry is to be rid of the conceit of chivalry; giving up affectation is to be finished with all attachments; and generosity is to leave the world to the worldly." *(Ibid)*

67. Nuri: "Sufism is to sacrifice the ego's share for the sake of God's share." *(Tadhkerat al-awliyā')*

68. Nuri: "Sufism is war against the world and friendship with the Lord." *(Ibid)*

69. Abu Mohammad Rovaym: "Sufism is based on three qualities: sticking to poverty, realizing true generosity by preferring (God and His creatures above oneself), and abandoning all personal initiative and choice." *(Resalāt al-Qoshayri)*

70. Rovaym: "Sufism is abandoning oneself to God on God's terms." *(Al-Loma')* Ebn 'Atā' meant the same thing when he said, "Sufism is to be 'abandoned' to God, such that one goes whichever way He pulls." *(Sharh Ta'arrof)*

71. Rovaym: "Sufism is ceasing to consider one thing better than another." *(Tarā'eq al-haqā'eq)*

72. Abu Mohammad Morta'esh, upon being asked to define Sufism, replied, "Obscurity, complication and concealment." *(Nafahāt al-ons)*

73. Morta'esh: "Sufism is beauty of character." *(Kashf al-mahjub)*

74. Morta'esh: "Sufism is a state that delivers the Sufi from idle chatter and leads him to God, the Bestower of Favor, and then removes him completely, so that God remains and he himself becomes nothing." *(Tadhkerat al-awliyā')*

75. Mamshād Dinavari: "Sufism is purity of the innermost consciousness, acting on God's pleasure, and being the companion of people but without self-will." *(Ibid)*

76. Dinavari: "Sufism is to make a show of wealth, thereby choosing anonymity in that people will not recognize you (as a darvish) and to disdain all that cannot be used (on the Path)." *(Tadhkerat al-awliyā')*

77. 'Ali ebn Sahl Esfahāni: "Sufism is to wash one's hands of 'other-than-God' and to be empty of all but Him." *(Nafahat al-ons)*

78. Abu Mohammad Jorayri: "Sufism is to watch closely *(morāqabah)* one's states and to maintain *adab* (the correct manners of the Path)." *(Resālat al-Qoshayri)*

79. Jorayri also said that Sufism is "to assume all exalted virtues, leaving all lowly dispositions behind." *(al-Loma')*

80. Abu 'Amr Demashqi: "Sufism is to contemplate created existence as a fault, or rather to ignore all imperfections by gazing upon that which transcends them." *(Nafahat al-ons)*

Hojviri quotes this saying as, "Sufism is to gaze upon created existence as imperfection, or rather to disregard it altogether!" He explains, "If one is still gazing at imperfection, one's human attributes after all still survive; if one disregards imperfection, these attributes have been annihilated, for the "gaze" itself belongs to created existence. When no such existence survives, no gazing is possible. This disregard is a God-given insight; he who no longer sees through himself sees through God." *(Kashf al-mahjub)*

81. Abu Bakr Kattāni: "Sufism is noble character; if anyone outranks you in that, he outranks you in purity as

well." *(Resalāt al-Qoshayri)* (The author of the *Kashf al-mahjub* ascribes this saying to Mohammad ebn 'Ali ebn al-Husayn ebn 'Ali ebn Abi Tāleb, a great-grandson of 'Ali, but in place of the word "purity" he uses "Sufism.")

82. Abol-Hasan Mozayyen: "Sufism is to be led by God." *(Resalāt al-Qoshayri)*

83. Abu 'Abdollah Khafif: "Sufism is patience in the face of fate, acceptance from God's hand, and voyages over deserts and mountains." *(Tadhkerat al-awliyā')*

84. 'Amr ebn 'Othman Makki, when asked about Sufism, replied, "The servant is busy each moment with what is most appropriate to that moment." *(Resalāt al-Qoshayri and al-Loma')*

85. Abo'l-Hasan Qannād, asked for a definition of Sufism, replied, "Letting go of (one's own) station and constant Union." *(Al-Loma')*

86. Qannād: "Sufism is a name for a suit of clothes, but Sufis have no uniform states and stations!" *(Al-Loma')*

87. Mohammad ebn 'Ali Qassāb: "Sufism is noble character manifest at a noble time by a noble man among noble folk."

88. Somnun Mohebb, asked to define Sufism, replied, "You own nothing, nothing owns you." *(Al-Loma')*

89. Abu 'Abdollāh Rudbāri: "Sufism is to abandon affectation but make use of wit and to give up the pursuit of rank." *(Nafahāt al-ons)*

90. Abu 'Amr Najid: "Sufism is patience with God's com-

mands and prohibitions." *(Tadhkerat al-awliyā)* (Ansāri has been credited with another version of this saying: "Sufism is patience with God's commands and prohibitions such that the Sufi does not overstep them.") *(Rasā'el-e Ansāri)*

91. Mohammad ebn Ahmad al-Moqri: "Sufism means that one's states are straightened by God." The author of the *Kashf al-mahjub* explains, "The Sufi's states do not cause his innermost consciousness to deviate or fall into the crooked." *(Kashf al-mahjub)*

92. Abu Hafs Haddād Nayshāburi: "Sufism, all of it, is various forms of *adab*. Each moment, each station, and each state has its proper action. To adhere to the behavior that is proper to the moment is to attain the measure of the great Sufis; he who fails in this *adab* can never imagine nearness to God, nor that God might accept his behavior." *(Kashf al-mahjub)*

93. 'Ali ebn Bondār Sayrafi: "Sufism is blindness for the sake of God, both inwardly and outwardly." That is, according to the author of *Kashf al-mahjub*, "The Sufi is blind to himself, outwardly and inwardly, but sees all things as God." *(Kashf al-mahjub)*

94. Ebn al-Jalā': "Sufism is a reality without delineation." The author of the *Kashf al-mahjub* explains, "Delineation typifies the affairs of creation, but reality belongs only to God. Since Sufism involves turning away from all created things, naturally it has no delineation." *(Kashf al-mahjub)*

95. Abu Solaymān Dārāni defined Sufism by saying, "Things happen to the Sufi that no one knows save God, and he is ever with God such that no one knows but God." *(Tadhkerat al-awliyā')*

96. Sahl ebn 'Abdollāh Tostari: "Sufism is to eat sparingly, to be at ease with God, and to flee from creatures." *(Ibid)*

97. Asked to define the "Science of Sufism," Qaysari replied that it was "the science of God's Names and Attributes and the loci in which they manifest themselves; the states of the Beginning and End (that is, creation and resurrection); the world's realities and their return to a single Reality, the One Essence; and knowledge of the path of spiritual travail and warfare, waged that the soul might be freed from the bonds of individuality, returned to its origin, and qualified by the attributes of nondelimitation and universality." *(Sharh al-Tā'iyyeh)*

98. Shaykh-e Bahā'i: "The science of Sufism deals with the One Essence and with Its Names and Attributes inasmuch as they link the loci of their outward manifestation, together with all related phenomena, to the Divine Essence. Thus, the *subject* of this science is the One Essence and its beginningless and eternal Attributes. The *questions* it investigates include: (1) the emanation of multiplicity from the One Essence and its return thence, (2) the loci of manifestation as reflections of the Divine Names and Attributes, (3) the return of God's people to Him, (4) their wayfaring, spiritual warfare and ascetic practices, and (5) the fruits of each work and remembrance and their actual results in both this world and the next. Finally, the *principles* of this science are the knowledge of its definition and aim, and the technical terminology of the Sufis."

99. "It has been said that Sufism is purification of the heart from conformity with the habits of creatures; separation from those moral qualities belonging to 'nature' (the imprints and impressions of the lower world) by transforming them, purging them of deviations, and basing them upon a 'golden mean' without either exaggeration or neglect; wip-

31

ing out all human attributes through spiritual warfare, ascetic practice, and involvement with spiritual attributes;
emulating the angels in constant obedience and eschewing
all rebellion; learning the sciences of Reality, those which
do not vanish with the world's passing away (i.e., the science of God and His Words); following the Prophet in the
Shari'at, and 'Ali, the saint and heir of the Prophet, in the
Tariqat, which is for the Sufi the anchor of all welfare."
(Tarā'eq al-haqā'eq)

100. "It has been said that Sufism consists of moral qualities approved (by God), such that in every state the Sufi is
content with God's good pleasure." *(Kashf al-mahjub)*

101. "The science of Sufism is never exhausted, for it
springs from God's generosity rather than quantity, and
from inspiration rather than memorization." *(Sharh-e
ta'arrof)*

102. Sohravardi: "A great sage was asked about Sufism
and replied, 'Its beginning is God, but it has no end!'"
(Majmu'e-ye āthār-e fārsi)

103. One of the masters once gave the following tripartite
definition of Sufism. As a science, he said, "It is purification of the heart of all opacity; it is to behave well towards
all and to follow the Prophet in the Shari'at." In the language of spirituality, he said, "It is the lack of attachment,
freedom from the bondage of (human) attributes, and the
acquisition of independence through the Creator of the
heavens." In the language of God, he said, "He singled
them out *(safā)* for purity *(safā')* from their own attributes,
and then purified them *(saffā')* of their own purity. Thus,
they were called 'Sufis.'" *(al-Loma')*

104. "Sufism in the beginning is knowledge and in the

middle, practice of heart and body. Its end is the gift of gnostic sciences and verities." *(Tarā'eq al-haqā'eq)*

105. This *faqir* (the author) says, "Sufism is to flee 'other-than-God' and to take repose in His shadow."

106. Again, "Sufism is to walk towards God on God's feet."

107. Again, "Sufism is to abandon one's own opinion and submit to God's will."

108. And finally, "Sufism is to know One, desire One, see One, and become One."

WORDS OF THE MASTERS
CONCERNING THE TERM "SUFI"

1. Abu 'Ali Rudbāri: "The Sufi wears wool *(suf)* upon purity *(safā)* and forces his ego *(nafs)* to taste the cruelty (of being ignored); he leaves the world behind and travels the way of Mohammad." *(Sharh-e Ta'arrof)*

2. Dhon-Nun Mesri: "The Sufi is one who never tires in striving nor becomes disturbed by being deprived." *(Al-Loma')*

3. Dhon-Nun: "They have chosen God over all, so God chooses them over all." *(Ibid)*

4. Dhon-Nun: "When the Sufi speaks, he reveals the realities of his state; he says nothing which he is not. When he is silent, his conduct itself expresses his state and speaks of his detachment." *(Tadhkerat al-awliyā')*

5. Jonayd was asked, "Who are the Sufis?", and replied, "They are God's chosen creatures; He conceals them or reveals them as He desires." *(al-Loma')*

6. On another occasion, Jonayd answered the same question by saying, "The Sufis are members of one family into which no one else enters." *(Resālat al-Qoshayri)*

7. Jonayd: "The Sufi is like the earth: refuse and ugliness are spilled upon it, but only beauty blossoms from it." *(Ibid)*

8. Jonayd: "The Sufi is like the earth, where godly and profligate alike may walk; like the clouds, which give shade to all things; or like the rain, which quenches all thirst." *(Ibid)*

9. Jonayd: "The Sufi's heart, like Abraham's, is secure from the world, obeying God's commands; his submission is that of Ishmael; his grief that of David; his poverty that of Jesus, his patience that of Job; his yearning (for God) that of Moses when he called upon God; and his sincerity that of Mohammad." *(Tadhkerat al-awliyā')*

10. Jonayd: "The Sufis are those who stand in God, knowing none but Him." *(Ibid)*

11. Jonayd: "The word Sufi derives from 'wool' *(suf)* which has three letters: s, w and f. 'S' stands for *sabr* (patience), *sedq* (truthfulness), and *safā'* (purity); 'W' for *wadd* (love), *werd* (litany), and *wafā'* (faithfulness); 'F' stands for *fard* (detachment), *faqr* (poverty) and *fanā* (annihilation in God)." *(Tarā'eq al-haqā'eq)*

12. Abol-Hasan Hosri: "The Sufi's ecstatic consciousness is his very being; his attributes are but a veil; (as

the Prophet said) 'Whosoever knows himself, knows his Lord.' " *(Tadhkerat al-awliyā')*

13. Hosri: "When the Sufi has been annihilated from afflictions, he does not return to them; when he lifts his face unto the Lord, he does not fall from the Lord; and the events of time do not touch him." *(Ibid)*

14. Hosri: "The Sufi does not gain existence after non-existence, nor non-existence after existence." That is, according to the *Kashf al-mahjub,* "Whatever he finds he never loses, and that which he loses he never finds. His finding never knows not-finding; his not-finding never possesses a finding."

15. Sarrāj: "I asked Hosri, 'Who, in your opinion, is the Sufi?' He replied, 'The one whom earth does not carry nor the heavens overshadow.' By this, Hosri meant that although the Sufi may walk upon earth and under heaven, it is not earth that upholds him nor the sky that shades him, but rather God." *(Al-Loma')*

16. Kattāni: "The Sufi is one who sees his very obedience to God as a sin for which he must beg forgiveness (for his obedience arises from himself, not from God)." *(Tadhkerat al-awliyā')*

17. Nuri: "The Sufi is at rest with non-existence and generous with existence." *(Resalāt al-Qoshayri)*

18. Nuri: "The tribe of the Sufis has been freed from the darkness of human nature, purified from the ego's poison and delivered from self-will; the Sufis are at rest with God in the front rank and loftiest degree and have fled from all but Him; they neither own nor are owned." *(Ibid)*

19. Nuri: "The Sufi is tied to nothing, and nothing is tied to him." *(Kashf al-Mahjub)* and *(Tadhkerat al-awliyā')*

20. Nuri: "The Sufi is one who listens to the spiritual concert *(samā')* and prefers it above all things (literally, "above all secondary causes")." *(al-Loma')*

21. Qannād: "When the servant realizes the station of servitude, and when God loves him sincerely *(sāfā)* until he is purified from the darkness of human nature, he comes to reside in the way-stations of the Truth and becomes one with the statutes of the Shari'at. Thus is he a Sufi, for he is 'loved sincerely' *(sufi)*." *(al-Loma')*

22. Qannād: " 'Sufi' is derived from *safā* (purity), which means standing before God in faithfulness at every moment." *(Ibid)*

23. Shaykh Abu Sa'id: "The Sufi does what he does for God's pleasure, that everything God does may please him." *(Asrar al-tawhid)*

24. "Abu Sa'id was asked, 'How is it God can be seen, but not the Sufi?' He answered, 'Because God is Being, and what *is* can be seen; but the Sufi is non-being, and non-being cannot be seen.' " *(Ibid)*

25. Beshr Hāfi: "The Sufi is one who has purified *(sāfi)* his heart for God; and some have said that he is the person who purifies his conduct for Him." *(Sharh-e ta'arrof)*

26. Bondār ebn al-Hosayn as-Sufi: "God has chosen the Sufi for Himself, for His friend; He causes the Sufi to shun his own ego *(nafs)* and does not allow him to slide back to self-centered activity, affection, and pretension." *(Ibid)*

27. Tostari: "The Sufi is purified of darkness, filled with meditation, separated from the creatures, joined to God. For him, mud and gold have equal value." *(Ibid)*

28. Tostari was asked, "Among all people, whom should we make our companions?" He answered, "The Sufis, for they never consider what is nothing as something important, and they manage to find a justification for everything; thus, they'll provide you with an alibi for every occasion!" *(Ibid)*

29. Tostari: "The Sufi is one who will let his blood be shed with impunity and who considers his property up for grabs." *(Resālat al-Qoshayri)*

30. Abu Abdollāh 'Abdol-Wāhed ebn Zayd was asked, "Who, in your opinion, are the Sufis?" He answered, "Those who, controlling their aspirations with their intellects, devote their hearts to these aspirations and take refuge from their own egos *(nafs)* in their master. These are the Sufis." *(al-Loma')*

31. Ebn al-Jalā': "The Sufi cannot be defined scientifically, but any faqir who is disengaged from phenomena, who is placelessly with God and whom God does not hold back from the knowledge of any place, may be called a Sufi." *(Ibid)*

32. Abol-Hasan Kharaqāni: "Patched cloak and prayer carpet do not make a Sufi, nor practice and custom; the Sufi is he who is not." *(Nafahāt al-ons)*

33. Kharaqāni: "The Sufi is a day without need of the sun, a night without need of moon and stars; he is a nothingness without need of existence." *(Ibid)*

34. Kharaqāni: "Till you are not, all of you will be. God says, 'I have created all these creatures, except the Sufi.'" 'Attār explains, "The non-existent is not created. This can also mean that the Sufi belongs to the spiritual world, not the physical." *(Tadhkerat al-awliyā')*

35. Kharaqāni: "The Sufi is a dead body, a non-existent heart, and a soul scorched away." *(Ibid)*

36. Shebli was asked, "Why are these folk called 'Sufis'?" He answered, "Because something of themselves remains; if this were not so, it would be impossible to name them!" *(al-Loma')*

37. Shebli: "The Sufis are children in God's lap." *(Resālat al-Qoshayri)*

38. Shebli: "Sufis are cut off from creatures, connected to God. In His words to Moses, 'I have chosen thee for Myself' *(Koran, XX: 41),* God cut him off from every 'other' and then said to him, 'Thou shalt not see Me!' *(Koran, VII: 139)*" *(Resālat al-Qoshayri)*

39. Abu Sa'id has quoted Shebli as saying, "The Sufi is not a Sufi till all creation has become his household." In other words, Abu Sa'id explains, "The Sufi looks on all people with compassion's eye, considering it his duty to bear their burdens, since everything and all are equally subject to fate and the Divine will." *(Asrār al-tawhid)*

40. Shebli: "In this world and the next, the Sufi sees nothing but God." *(Kashf al-Mahjub)*

41. Abu Mohammad Rāsebi: "The Sufi is not a Sufi till the earth refuses to carry him, the sky to shade him, and

the creatures to accept him, so that in every state his refuge is God." *(Nafahāt al-ons)*

42. Abu Bakr Vāseti: "The Sufi does not speak subjectively; his inner consciousness is illuminated through meditation." *(Tadhkerat al-awliyā')*

43. Abu 'Abdollah Mohammad ebn Fazl: "The Sufi is undisturbed by tribulation and unmoved by signs of grace." *(Ibid)*

44. Morta'esh: "The aspiration of the Sufi does not outreach his stride." In other words, according to the *Kashf al-mahjub,* "The Sufi's awareness extends even to his feet; his heart is present with his body, even as his body with his heart. This is a sign of presence without absence. Some say, 'The Sufi is absent from himself but present with God,' but no! In truth, he is present both with himself and God alike. This is 'concentration within concentration.' If you still perceive the self, you cannot be truly absent from the self; but when all perception vanishes, there is presence without absence." *(Kashf al-Mahjub)*

45. Abu Torāb Nakhshabi: "Nothing besmirches the Sufi; rather, all things are purified through him." *(Resālat al-Qoshayri)*

46. Abu Sa'id Kharrāz: "The Sufi has been purified by his Lord and fully illuminated; as a result of his remembrance, he is the very essence of joy." *(Tadhkerat al-awliyā')*

47. One of the masters said, "When the Sufi is presented with two beautiful states or virtues, he goes with the higher and more beautiful." *(al-Loma')*

48. Sarrāj: "The Sufi's conduct is purified for God, such

that his nobility is purified for God by God." *(Ibid)*

49. Sarrāj: "If anyone should ask you what the Sufis are really like, say that they are those who know God and His law, who practice what God has taught them, who have fulfilled what God intended for them, who are ecstatic at their realization, and who are annihilated in that which gave them their ecstasy—just as all ecstatics are annihilated in ecstasy." *(Ibid)*

50. "Sufis are called Sufis because their hearts are illuminated and their outward manifestation is pure." *(Sharh-e ta'arrof)*

51. Abu Ya'qub Susu: "You cannot move a Sufi by stealing from him, nor does the search (for possessions) disturb him." The author of the *Sharh-e ta'arrof* explains, "In other words, if something is taken from him, he does not bother to seek it." *(Sharh-e ta'arrof)*

52. "One of the masters once said, 'He who is purified by love is pure *(sāf)*, but he who is loved sincerely by the Beloved Himself (i.e., who is drowned in love and lost to everything but the Beloved), that one becomes a Sufi.' " *(Kashf al-mahjub)*

53. Qoshayri: "The Sufi is like someone suffering from fever. At first he raves deliriously, but at the end he falls silent, for when you reach the station of 'consolidation' you are struck dumb." *(Ibid)*

54. This faqir (the author) says, "The Sufi is like the earth of submission from which the seed of love, planted by God in his heart, may sprout and reach the air of the Divine Essence."

55. And again, this faqir says, "The Sufi is no one. How can 'no one' be defined?"

MA' REFAT

Knowledge of God

THE literal translation of the Arabic word *ma'refat* is "knowledge." Although as a technical term in Sufism it bears the same significance, it also implies a knowledge that is preceded by meditation and that allows of no doubt. According to some Sufis, *ma'refat* is comprehension or knowledge of "the thing itself," of essential knowledge. In this essay, however, the word is used to mean true knowledge of God.

A drop of spray cannot engulf the sea nor can the part comprehend the whole; thus, without doubt, man cannot know God in a way that befits Him. The best proof of this is God's own saying, "They measure not God with His true measure" *(Koran,* VI: 92; XXXIX: 67); and, as the Prophet has said, "We have not known Thee according to Thy true measure."

Of course, with Divine help and grace, one may know God's attributes, at least to the extent of one's capacity. However, no one can know God's Essence, His very Self, through his own limited selfhood. As 'Ali has said, "I know God by God; I know 'other-than-God' by God's light."

No one makes his way to God
  under his own feeble power.
Whoever walks to His lane
  walks with His feet.

Maghrebi

No one can know Him through one's own self;
only through Him can His Essence be known.

Sanā'i

Thus have the Sufis claimed, "As long as you are yourself, you cannot know Him. When your 'you-ness' vanishes and His 'He-ness' appears, you will know Him through Him."

This 'me' is renewed by Him, moment by moment;
When this 'me' is lost to me, Him I see.

Rumi

Or, in the words of Bābā Tāher Hamadāni, "He who sees his own being intrude into the station of knowledge is yet, even in his knowledge, an ignoramus."

THE ROLE OF REASON ('AQL) IN THE ACQUISITION OF KNOWLEDGE

The intellect or reason has a temporal origin, and that which is limited by temporality cannot possess the power to know the Eternal. Reason is a faculty for acquiring knowledge, for receiving whatever information God might send us, and ultimately for coming to know that we do not know. This last realization constitutes the pinnacle of the-

45

oretical knowledge based upon the intellect.

The role of the intellect or reason has been clarified numerous times by Sufi masters. For example, when they asked Abol-Hasan Nuri, "What is the proof of God?" he replied, "God." "Then what is the role of the intellect?" they asked. "The intellect," Nuri replied, "is impotent, and the impotent can only prove that which, like itself, is impotent." *(Sharh-e ta'arrof)* According to Ebn'Atā', "The intellect is the organ of servitude, not that by which Lordship is perceived." *(Sharh-e ta'arrof)* And Nuri has said, "There is no proof of God but God. We seek knowledge *('elm)* only that we may serve Him." *(Kashf al-mahjub)*

Exoteric scholars and religious jurisprudents have used the term *ma'refat* to mean correct theoretical knowledge *('elm)* of God. Sufi masters, however, have considered *ma'refat* to be a correct spiritual state reached *through* God. Sound theoretical knowledge may be a means of attaining *ma'refat,* but it cannot be its direct cause; only God's grace and kindness can bring about such real knowledge. The unaided intellect is ignorant, and no mere "intellectual" can understand this limitation. If the intellect is thus unknowing of itself, how could it come to know other than itself?

The Sufis believe that intellectual or rational demonstration cannot serve as the cause of true knowledge. "The very first stage of logical demonstration," they say, "is a turning away from God. 'Demonstration' implies reflection upon 'other,' but real knowledge is to turn away from 'other-than-God.' " *(Sharh-e ta'arrof)*

> *The logician's leg is made of wood,*
> *and wooden legs are clumsy.*
>
> Rumi

Hojviri has said:

46

By custom, demonstration is used to prove the existence of those things whose existence one seeks to prove. But knowledge of God defies all custom; it is, in fact, the unending bewilderment of the intellect. There is no way to earn the turning of His Grace toward the servant, and no proof for the servant except His Bounty and Kindness. Such 'proof' comes only from the opening of the heart, from the treasury of the Unseen. *(Kashf al-mahjub)*

Even the "universal intellect" of the Prophet declared, "Glory to Him Who has given the creatures no way to knowledge of Him other than the very incapacity for that knowledge!" If this is true of Mohammad, then the duty of the particular intellects of ordinary beings becomes quite obvious.

THE STAGES OF KNOWLEDGE

Sufi masters have discussed various levels and types of knowledge, each speaking in light of his own spiritual station and intuitive perception. Ansāri, for example, has said:

There are two kinds of knowledge (of God): that of the vulgar and that of the elect. The knowledge of the vulgar is by hearsay, but that of the elect comes from direct vision. The former springs from the fountain of Divine Generosity, but the latter is the very Existent Himself. *(Tabaqāt as-sufiyah)*

According to Hojviri:

Knowledge of God is of two kinds: doctrinal knowledge *(ma'refat-e elmi)* and knowledge gained through spiritual experience *(ma'refat-e hāli)*. God says, "I have not created the jinn and mankind except to worship Me," *(Koran,* LI: 56), in other words, "except to know Me." Knowledge is the life of the heart through God, consciousness turned away from all but God. A man's value is measured by his knowledge; he who lacks it is worth nothing. *(Kashf al-mahjub)*

Another author says:

Perfect knowledge is actualized for the adept when he attains total annihilation *(fanā),* followed by subsistence (baqā), followed by a return to the station of (theoretical) knowledge *('elm).* Such a person achieves the station of summoning humanity to God: the station of a prophet or vice-regent to a prophet.

The adept, at the beginning of his wayfaring, derives his first true knowledge from the contemplation or direct perception of the Divine Names as they are manifested in his own existence. The second or intermediate knowledge derives from his perception of the manifestation of these Names themselves as God's own Attributes; that is, he recognizes this manifestation as belonging to God. As the Sufis have said, "The first stage of knowledge is to affirm the Attributes with respect to the locus of manifestation which becomes described by them," that is to say, the human spirit. In the third and final stage of knowledge, the adept comes to understand his own ignorance of the realities of these Attributes (i.e., he is ignorant of the Essence, which is their source). One might say the final stage is to *become ignorant,* blinded by the sunrise of the realities of the

Attributes and of the knowledge of God. *(Sharh-e kalimāt-e Bābā Tāher)*

Abu Mansur Mo'ammer of Isfahan has said:

Knowledge is of three sorts: of primordial nature, of increase, and of election. When the seeker affirms God's unity, he is established in the knowledge of primordial nature. If he strives sincerely, waging spiritual warfare, he is established in the knowledge of increase. The knowledge of election derives from the well-spring of generosity; spiritual endeavor follows upon it. *(Tabaqāt as-sufiyah)*

In the words of Ebn 'Atā:

There are two sorts of knowledge: that of the Truth and that of Reality. The first is the recognition of God's Oneness through His Names and Attributes. However, man has no access to the second sort of knowledge, of Reality Itself, for His Eternity is unreachable, his Lordship actualized. God says, "They comprehend Him not in knowledge." *(Koran, XX: 110)* Man is not capable of such knowledge, can see no boundaries to His Immensity and His Thusness, which outstrip all comprehension. In but an atom of this hugeness, heaven and earth are swallowed. "They measure not God with His true measure." *(Koran, VI: 92) (Tabaqāt as-sufiyah)*

Another version of Ebn 'Atā's saying is related as follows:

Knowledge is of two kinds: of the Truth and of Reality. Knowledge of the Truth consists of the affirmation of divine Oneness through those

49

Attributes which He has made manifest. Knowledge of Reality is not attained by every knower, however, because of the inaccessibility of Eternity and the actualization of Lordship. The 'inaccessibility of Eternity' is explained in the saying, "There is no path toward the Eternal *(samad)* through affirmation." That is, there is no path to the Eternal, which is the All-subjugating Power of Force, Wrath and Conquest. *(Sharh-e ta'arrof)*

According to Ansāri:

Knowledge of demonstration is for mere hirelings; argumentative (intellectual) knowledge is for wretches; knowledge of instrumentality is for the destitute; knowledge mixed with optimism is for beggars; when mixed with fear, it is for neurotics. O where is knowledge drowned in the profession of God's Unity *(tawhid)? That* indeed is knowledge! *(Tabaqāt as-sufiyah)*

Ansāri has also said:

Knowledge is comprehension of the thing in itself as it is. There are three sorts of knowledge: knowledge of Attributes and Descriptions; knowledge of the Essence in which the distinction between the Attributes and the Essence is transcended; and knowledge absorbed into the very Source of all knowing. This last cannot be reached through logic nor demonstrated by evidence; nor can it be attained by means of the knowledge of primordial nature, of evidence, contemplation, estimation, judgement, or investigation. *(Tabaqāt as-sufiyah)*

Dhon-Nun has defined knowledge in the following way:

Knowledge is of three kinds: first, knowledge of the profession of Unity, which belongs to the ordinary believers; second, knowledge of argument and proof, which pertains to the philosophers, literati and scholars; third, knowledge of the Attributes of Oneness, which belongs to God's Friends, the saints who contemplate Him in their hearts till He reveals to them what He reveals to none other in the world. *(Tadhkerat al-awliyā')*

In the words of Jonayd:

Knowledge is of two kinds: of disclosure and of instruction. In the first, God discloses Himself to men, so occupying them with Himself that they ignore all signs and evidence. In the second, He gives them knowledge that they may know Him, instructing them in evidence, arguments, and signs that they may gain access to him. . . .

Disclosure means that He acquaints them with Himself so that they know Him through Him, ascribing to Himself those things with which He acquaints them, so that they know things through Him, not Him through things. In knowledge through *instruction,* however, He unveils the traces of His power on the world's horizons and in the human body; He creates within men a sentiment in light of which creation reveals to them its Creator. This is the knowledge of ordinary believers, while the first (knowledge of *disclosure)* is that of the elect. In reality, no one knows Him except through Him. As Mohammad Vāse' put it, "I see nothing without God in it"; and as someone else said, "I see nothing without God *before* it!" *(Sharh-e ta'arrof)*

51

Again, Ebn 'Atā' has said:

God allows ordinary folk to know Him through His
creation: "Will they not regard the camel, how it was
created? And heaven, how it was raised? And the
mountains, how they were set up? And earth, how it
was outstretched?" *(Koran,* LXXXVIII: 17-20) But as
for the elect, they know Him through His Words and
His Attributes: "Will they not then ponder on the
Koran?" (Koran, IV: 82), "And we send down, of the
Koran, that which is a healing and mercy to the
believers," *(Koran,* XVII: 82), and "To God belong
the Names Most Beautiful, so call Him by them."
(Koran, VII: 180) As for the prophets, He makes
them knowers of His Essence: "Even so We have
revealed to thee (Mohammad) a Spirit of Our
bidding; thou knewest not what the Book was, nor
belief, but we made it a light whereby We guide
whom We will of Our servants. And thou, surely
thou shalt guide onto a straight path." *(Koran,* XLII:
52), and "Hast thou not seen thy Lord, how He has
stretched out the shadow?" *(Koran,* XXV: 45) The
common folk proceed from the act to the Agent; the
elect proceed from the Attributes and Names to the
Named, to the Possessor of Attributes; and the
prophets proceed from Essence to Essence. *(Sharh-e
ta'arrof)*

Some Sufis hold that knowledge has three stages: a
beginning, a middle, and an end:

The beginning is that the Cause is (logically)
demonstrated through the effect, the Maker through
the made. This, the knowledge of ordinary folk, is

knowledge in name only, the mere imprint of knowledge without its reality.

The middle stage is knowledge attained through contemplation of the Known. This is the knowledge of the elect; it may truly be ascribed to its possessor, unlike the first sort of knowledge, which is ascribed to its possessor only linguistically, as it were, and not in reality.

The last is unitive knowledge, attained by the union of knower and known through annihilation in Him. This knowledge is reserved for the most elect of the elect, those who realize that the realities of knowledge cannot be comprehended as they really exist in themselves, since only the eternal and beginningless knowledge of God Himself can encompass them. *(Sharh-e kalemāt)*

WORDS OF THE MASTERS ON KNOWLEDGE OF GOD *(MA'REFAT)*

1. Abol-Hasan Mozayyen: *"Ma'refat* is that you see in God the perfection of Lordship and in yourself servant-hood, that you know God as the First of all things, and that you know that to Him all things return, each thing depending on Him for its sustenance." *(Tabaqāt as-sufiyah)*

2. Ebn Yazdānyān: *"Ma'refat* is the correct knowledge of God, certitude, vision with the heart's eye of what is with God, what He has promised and stored away." *(Ibid)*

3. *"Ma'refat* is the heart's realization of God's Oneness." *(Ibid)*

4. *"Ma'refat* is the manifestation of the realities and the union of witness and witnessed." *(Ibid)*

53

5. Bāyazid: *"Ma'refat* of the divine Essence is but ignorance; the science of the reality of *ma'refat* is mere bewilderment. Whatever they say of Him is sheer idolatry; those who say most are farthest from the truth." *(Ibid)*

6. *"Ma'refat* is based either on demonstration—the logical demonstration of God's existence by His signs—or on contemplation, which demonstrates His existence by Himself as the Displayer of signs. The latter is called 'The Proof of Saints.'" *(Kashshāf)*

7. Hojviri: "God guides His servants to Himself as He knows and desires, and for them opens the gate of knowledge." *(Kashf al-mahjub)*

8. Tostari: *"Ma'refat* is knowledge of one's own ignorance. The closer one gets to Him, the more overpowering becomes His Immensity and the more one gains in knowledge of ignorance. Bewilderment is heaped on bewilderment, and from the knower's heart comes the cry, 'My Lord, increase my bewilderment in Thee!'" *(Mesbāh al-hedāyah)*

9. Shebli: *"Ma'refat* is endless bewilderment." *(Sharh-e ta'arrof)*

10. Ghazzāli: "The lights of knowledge shine upon the heart from the World of the (Spiritual) Kingdom *(malakut)*, for the heart is also of that realm. But as for those traces of effects manifest within the heart, those are from the World of Invincibility *(jabarut)*, which (on the microcosmic level) is in fact the human breast." *(Arba'in)*

11. Hojviri: "When the reality of *ma'refat* appears within the knower's heart, the tyranny of opinion, doubt, and hesitation is overthrown; the rule of *ma'refat* conquers his

senses and self-will, such that all he does, says, and sees falls within the circle of God's command." *(Kashf al-mahjub)*

12. Abu Sa'id Abel-Khayr was once asked, "What is *ma'refat?*" He replied, "It is what children say to each other; first wipe your nose, then you can talk to me!" *(Asrār al-tawhid)*

13. Abu Sa'id reported, "Bāyazid used to say, 'God is alone and must be sought in aloneness; how will you find him with paper and ink?' " *(Ibid)*

14. Shebli: "One of the signs of *ma'refat* is that one sees oneself in the grasp of divine Might, flowing with the flow of divine Power." *(Tabaqāt as-sufiyah)*

15. Sari Saqati (quoted by Bāyazid): "Whosoever knows Him desires nothing, either from Him or from anything or anyone else." *(Ibid)*

16. Abu Hafs: "As soon as I came to know Him, neither truth nor falsehood entered my heart again." *(Ibid)*

17. Abu Bakr Vāseti: "If they knew Him, they wouldn't love Him!" This seemingly paradoxical statement is explained by Ansāri in the following way, "True knowledge leaves no trace in the knower of any attributes or qualities whereby he could love God (in the sense of loving an 'other')." *(Ibid)*

18. "Both Jonayd and Kharrāz said, 'My greatest sin is my knowledge of Him.' In other words, I can only imagine I know Him, since no one can know Him as befits Him, in His true measure, in the scope of His Might." *(Ibid)*

19. Abu Sāleh was asked to define *ma'refat* and replied, "To follow the Known in speech, act, intention, and intellect." *(Ibid)*

20. Shebli once declared, "No one has known God." When asked how that could be, he answered, "If they knew Him, they would never busy themselves with other than Him." *(Ibid)*
    As Rumi put it:

> *Know that he who is called by God*
> *is unemployed in worldly affairs,*
> *For whoever's workload comes from God*
> *is received by Him and leaves business behind.*

21. Abu Tib Sāmeri: *"Ma'refat* is the dawning of truth on the innermost horizon of consciousness, brought about by the union of consciousness with the Divine lights." *(Tabaqāt as-sufiyah)*

22. Abu Bakr Qabbāni: "The reality of knowledge is the reality of the Known." *(Ibid)*

23. Abol-'Abbās Sayyāri was asked, "What is *ma'refat?*", and replied, "The innermost consciousness cut off from all but the thought of God, rather than its thinking of the ego *(nafs)." (Ibid)*

24. "Jonayd said that he who knows God will never be joyful. Shebli said that he who knows God will never grieve. Tostari said that he who knows God is drowned in the sea of grief and joy." *(Ibid)*

25. Abol-Hosayn Zanjāni: "Theory guides us in the accomplishment of works of obedience, while *ma'refat* guides

us past the dangers that may arise out of such works."
(Ibid)

26. Abol-'Abbās Sayyāri: *"Ma'refat* is the life of the heart *in* God and the life of the heart *with* God." *(Ibid)*

27. Ahmed Khadriyah: "True *ma'refat* is to love Him with the heart, invoke Him with the tongue, and cut off your will from all but Him." *(Tadhkerat al-awliyā)*

28. Solaymān Dārāni, asked to explain the reality of *ma'refat,* replied, "It is that one has but one desire in the two worlds." *(Ibid)*

29. "Dhon-Nun said that the reality of *ma'refat* is that God communicates to the inmost consciousness that to which the subtle lights of knowledge pertain; in other words, 'The sun can be seen only by the sun's light.'"
(Ibid)

30. It has been said that "He who knows God does not describe Him, and he who describes Him does not know Him." *(Sharh-e ta'arrof)* In other words, "Where there is vision is no discourse; where there is discourse, no vision."

31. "Fāres Baghdādi said, *'Ma'refat* is that the knower is consummated in contemplation of the known; the consummated one is he who is totally stripped of himself.' In other words, when the servant's conformity (with God) is perfected, his attributes are stripped from him; the contemplation of the known so overpowers his inmost consciousness that he is freed of all realities and attributes." *(Sharh-e ta'arrof)*

MA'REFAT ACCORDING TO ANSĀRI, THE PATRON SAINT OF HERAT

"God says, 'When they hear what has been sent down to the Messenger, thou seest their eyes overflow with tears because they know it to be the truth.' *(Koran, V: 83)*

"*Ma'refat* is the comprehension of the thing itself as it really is; there are three degrees of it, and a group associated with each degree.

"The first degree is the knowledge of the Attributes and descriptions of God, Whose Names we know from the *Koran* and Whose witnesses have appeared in the world; this knowledge we gain through the vision bestowed by the lights hidden in our inmost consciousness, by the burgeoning life-harvest of the intellect grown from the seeds of meditation, and by the awakened heart which joins reverence and the wisdom of experience. This is the knowledge of the ordinary believer; without it, there is no hope of realizing the pre-conditions of certainty.

"This first degree in turn rests upon three pillars: first, one must affirm a given Attribute through its *Koranic* Name without falling into the error of attributing creaturely characteristics to the Divinity. Second, having avoided this error, one must not fall into the opposite extreme by denying that God's Attributes are effectively manifested in the world; and finally, one must give up hope of perceiving the real nature of the Attributes, as well as striving to interpret them.

"The second degree is a knowledge of the Essence which transcends all distinction between Essence and Attributes. Such knowledge must arise from the science of the Divine All-Comprehensiveness (based on the premise that the Essence comprehends all Attributes). This knowledge is purified on the battlefield of annihilation, reaches its perfection in the science of subsistence, and approaches the very degree of All-Comprehensiveness (i.e. involves a spiritual state of near identity with It).

"This degree is also based on three pillars. One must identify one's own contemplative states with the Divine Attributes; one must identify one's own spiritual progress with the stages of the Path to God; and one must experience all words and explanations as guideposts along that Path. This is the knowledge of the elect, through which they familiarize themselves with the landscape of Reality.

"The third degree is a knowledge drowned in the sheer outpouring of divine knowledge. It cannot be reached by logical demonstration, nor pointed to by any evidence, nor, in effect, can it be attained by any means. Its three pillars are: contemplation of proximity, transcendence of all science, and the unclouded vision of All-Comprehensiveness. This is the knowledge of the elect of the elect." *(Manāzel as-sā'erin)*

"Knowledge has three gates: first, the recognition of existence and its homogeneity; second, the recognition of Power, Omniscience, and Beneficence; third, the recognition of right action, love, and proximity. The first is the gate of Islam, the second the gate of Faith, the third the gate of Sincerity.

"The pathway to the first gate passes through that eye that perceives the Creator's governance, His opening and closing of the affairs of Creation. The way to the second gate passes through the eye that beholds the Creator's wisdom in discernment. And the way to the third gate is through that eye that sees the Lord's kindness in rewarding merit and ignoring sin. This last gate is also the final battlefield of the knowers, the alchemy of lovers, the road of the elect, the highway of heart-adornment, increase of joy, and opening of love." *(Sad maydān)*

'EZZOD-DIN MAHMUD KĀSHĀNI ON *MA'REFAT*

"*Ma'refat* consists in recognizing an object as a whole and in principle within the forms of its particularized deployment . . . So knowledge of Lordship consists in recognizing the Divine Essence and Attributes in the particularized forms of the Divine Acts, phenomena and events (i.e., in Creation), this recognition taking place on the basis of a prior knowledge of God as True Existent and Absolute Agent. No one can properly be called a 'knower' until his theoretical profession of Unity becomes particularized and objectified (i.e., known in the objective and concrete world). In this way, he who adheres in theory to the profession of Unity sees and recognizes, without hesitation or deliberation, God as He-who-harms and He-who-gives-benefit, He-who-prevents and He-who-bestows, He-who-contracts and He-who-expands. This realization comes to him in the very forms of the particularized, ever-renewed, and conflicting events of the world, such as harm and benefit, prevention and bestowal, contraction and expansion. . . .

"Knowledge of God has various levels. The first: the knower must know that every phenomenon he perceives belongs to the Absolute Agent. Second: he should know exactly to which one of the Divine Attributes each of these phenomena can be traced. Third: he should know God's intention in each of these theophanic manifestations of the various Attributes. Fourth: he should recognize the Attributes of Divine Knowledge in the form of his own knowledge and should remove his own self from the circle of theory and knowledge (or rather, of phenomenal existence). Thus, when Jonayd was asked to define knowledge of God, he explained it as 'your ignorance when God's knowledge takes up residence.' When the questioner asked for further explanation, Jonayd replied, "God is the Knower and the Known." *(Mesbāh al-hedāyah)*

CHARACTERISTICS OF THE KNOWER OF GOD

The believer is one who stands with himself, while the knower is one who stands with his God.

(Ja'far as-Sādeq,
quoted in the
Tadhkerat al-awliyā')

Numerous well-known Sufis have expounded on the characteristics of the knower of God. The *Sharh-e ta'arrof* has preserved a number of these explanations, some of the most pertinent of which are presented below.

"Ebn Yazdānyār was once asked, 'When is the knower at God's shrine (lit., the "place of witnessing God")?' He replied, 'When the Witness Himself appears, annihilates the evidence, and the senses of the knower vanish and his sincerity is naughted.'

"Dhon-Nun was asked to describe the ultimate end of the knower's state; he replied, 'When he is now as he was before he was given existence.' That is to say, before man was created he possessed no free will and no ability to act. Now he is created, but if he is a knower, he will not know or see his own self and his own attributes, acts, and choices.

"On another occasion, Dhon-Nun was asked to describe the first degree reached by the knower. He replied, 'Bewilderment, then need, then union, then bewilderment!' In other words, bewilderment comes to the seeker first as a result of the love, favor, and blessing he receives from God, so much that his head spins with shame. Need comes

61

when he passes beyond his own shortcomings and inca-
pacities and sees God above his own servanthood; neces-
sarily then, he realizes himself helpless and incapable.
Union results from his being cut off from everything but
God. And finally, bewilderment returns again when he realizes that his incapacity and need were not the cause of
Union, since the discovery of God can have no 'cause.'
And so, the second bewilderment is that he becomes lost in
the uncharted wilderness of the profession of Unity, where
he loses his understanding, and his intellect is destroyed by
the greatness of God's power, His awesomeness and majesty. This 'uncharted wilderness,' this place of spinning
heads, in Arabic is *matāhāt,* which in turn is derived from
tih, 'a desert in which one loses the way.' A person who for
some reason becomes distracted or perplexed is referred to
as *tā'ih* (also from the same root). Thus Dhon-Nun went
on to say, 'Before reaching the profession of Unity, thought
loses itself in trackless wastes.' That is, he who seeks the
profession of Unity with his own thought will lose the way.
    "Abu Sawdā asked Hallāj if the knower possesses a
'moment.' This word, 'moment' or 'time' *(vaqt)* is a technical Sufi term meaning a spiritual state which appears
within the seeker's inmost consciousness and through
which he gains ease. So Abu Sawdā's question really was,
'Is it fitting for the knower to possess a moment through
which he gains ease? Hallāj replied, 'It is not fitting.' He
answered thus because such a moment would be an attribute of its possessor; he who finds satisfaction in his own
attribute is a companion of himself, and he who is a companion of himself is not God's companion. Such a moment, moreover, is something other than God, and the
knower cannot take ease in 'other-than-God.' Again, he
who 'takes ease' abandons aspiration, and to do this is to
turn away from God, which, as the Sufis say, is no better
than being an idolater.
    "Abu Sawdā then asked why this was so. Hallāj re-

plied, 'Because this moment is a state of pleasure (lit. a gap, breach, opening or relief of suffering), within which the possessor of the moment speaks of his sorrows. But knowledge is a flood which covers up the knower. He is drowned in the waves of knowledge from God, then comes to the surface again, and then is again taken under; the knower's moment is black and obscure.' In other words, aspiration cannot be checked, is not a deficiency of existence, and the existence of the object of aspiration has no limits. The knower never gains ease from the grief of aspiration, from his failure to reach the Object of aspiration. As he nearly perishes in the depth of his tribulation, God causes something to appear in his inmost consciousness and to occupy it and relieve him of his tribulation; he becomes 'absent' (loses consciousness in ecstasy), and one might say that his consciousness 'takes a breather.' He laments in his tribulation and weeps in his affliction, and thus finds 'ease.' So Hallāj maintains that when knowledge is correct, such a moment is not permissible to the knower, for this 'breather,' this moment of the inmost consciousness, is in effect a turning away from knowledge. To turn from knowledge is to turn from the Known, and 'whosoever turns away from God for even the blink of an eye will never be led to Him.'

"Moreover, consider the corpse of a drowned man, how when the waves flow, it flows with the waves. Now the tide brings the corpse to the surface, now submerges it in the depths. The corpse has no place to rest; the ocean has no shore; there is no sleeping and eating, no way for it to open its eyes and see, no way to open its mouth to breathe, no way to swim. And all this—a thousand waves of the ocean pounding this corpse—all this is nothing compared to the waves of Tremendousness, Majesty, and Awesomeness that crash upon the head of the knower. In his bewilderment, the knower's inmost consciousness is more helpless than that corpse in the ebb and flow of the sea.

63

And if he is not, then all his vaunted knowledge is but ignorance. If the vital spark of life is drowned in the ocean, how much less can the inmost consciousness bear the waves of Majesty and Awe? If the knower should still be able to discern a single atom of heaven or earth, he is not yet bewildered by the Divine Flood. Until he becomes such that no description will describe him, he is not worthy of his reputation for knowledge.

"Jonayd was asked, 'Who is the knower?' He answered, 'One might say he is neither the water nor the cup.' In other words, in whatever state he finds himself, he is appropriate to that state. His states differ; his choice has become God's choice, and God moves him from state to state in order that he should realize no mover exists but God. As the knower is being thus moved, he takes on the appearance of the Divine Attribute which is, as it were, moving him at that particular moment. Just so, water in a green cup appears green, in a white cup, white, and so on for any color, even though in fact the water retains its own hue. So also with the knower: his state and his moment are ordered by God. When God causes within his inmost consciousness a new state and moment to appear, his outward form takes on the appearance demanded by that state and moment, even though in truth the root remains in place, just as the water retains its original hue, despite the color given it by the cup. One moment requires the knower to be still, another to move; one gives cause for gratitude, another for complaint; one for patience, one for restlessness. Sometimes his moment moves him to companionship, sometimes to hermit-like seclusion; sometimes to speech, sometimes to silence. His 'outwardness' displays his conformity with the moment, while his 'inwardness' follows its own state.

"Hallāj declared that it is in this sense that one must understand the saying, 'The Sufi is the child of the moment.' That is, the knower's 'inwardness' and 'outwardness' both follow God, inasmuch as God continually moves his inwardness or causes it to rest, and his outwardness follows it in harmony. In this regard, Hallāj quoted Dhon-Nun, who, when asked about the knower, replied, 'He was here but he left.' In other words, one cannot find him in a single state for two moments together—for he is not his own mover. The knower has no choice, no permanent rest; that which gives him knowledge is God. This being the case, one should not describe him as being in a single, identifiable state; his attribute is descriptionlessness."

Many other explanations of the knower of God have been preserved in other famous Sufi texts, a few of which follow below.

Kharrāz: "Knowers are annihilated from self-governance by God's government." *(Tabaqāt as-sufiyah)*

Dhon-Nun, asked to describe the knower's activity, replied, "Gazing in every state on Him." *(Ibid)*

Abu Ghilān Samarqandi: "The knower understands God through God, the theoretician through 'other-than-God'—for all things point to His Oneness, and when the seeker reaches the Sought he no longer needs the pointers." *(Ibid)*

Rovaym: "The knower is a mirror; when he looks in it, His Lord manifests Himself to him." *(Ibid)*

Jonayd: "The knower's heart is unblemished, since with each breath he gazes upon his Lord." *(Ibid)*

Bāyazid: "Everyone has a state—except the knower, for his characteristics have been obliterated, and his traces have vanished in the traces of 'Other-than-He.' The Majestic One, through His Attributes, stands in the servant's place, and nothing remains of the servant which is not Him." Bāyazid also said, "While the servant is ignorant he is a knower, but his knowledge departs when his ignorance leaves him." *(Ibid)*

Dhon-Nun was asked about the knower's attribute and replied, "The knower is a seer with neither subjectivity nor objectivity, neither second-hand news nor first-hand vision—no attributes, no veils, and no unveilings. Knowers are not themselves and are not through themselves; when they are, they are through God. Their turnabout is through God's turning, their words are His, which have fallen upon their tongues, and their gaze is His, which has found its way to their eyes." *(Tadhkerat al-awliyā')*

Bāyazid: "The knower's fountain is not muddled by anything; all opacities that reach him become clear." *(Ibid)*

Abu Torāb Nakhshabi, when asked about the attribute of the knower, replied, "He is made impure by nothing, and all is purified through him." *(Ibid)*

Dhon-Nun: "The more he knows God, the greater and worse his bewilderment; the closer to the sun he becomes, the more bewildered, till he reaches a place where he ceases to be himself." *(Ibid)*

Kharrāz: "The stations of the People of Knowledge are bewilderment from utter need (for God), then joy, then annihilation, then wakefulness, then expectant subsistence. No one reaches farther than this." *(Tabaqāt as-sufiyah)*

THE DISTINCTION BETWEEN THE KNOWER AND SUFI

Imagine a ladder. The lowest rung is a theoretical knower who depends on the particular intellect, and the highest is a perfect Sufi. The knowers can be found between these two levels.

The more the knower depends on himself and his own knowledge, the lower the rung he occupies, but as he moves away from himself and his own knowledge, submitting more and more to God, he approaches the highest step. In reality then, the perfect knower and the perfect Sufi are one and the same.

PERFECT SUFI

THE KNOWERS

THEORETICAL KNOWER

TAWHID
Unity

TAWHID

Unity

TAWHID, or the "profession of God's Unity," is one of the basic principles of the *Shari'at,* and at the same time one of the final stations of the *Tariqat.* The followers of the *Shari'at* must have knowledge of it, while the wayfarers of the Path must consider it as their goal. Thus, what follows in this essay may be considered both a guide for the followers of the Law and a remembrance for the people of the Way. But, of course:

> *Who, in the midst of this*
> *crooked twisted world,*
> *am I?*
> *Like the letter alef (|),*
> *standing alone, I am adorned*
> *by nothing, nothing.*
> *Thou art the First,*
> *the Last—and I,*
> *in the middle,*
> *Am simply an*
> *inexplicable nothing,*
> *nothing!*

Rumi

THE MEANING OF THE WORD
TAWHID

The Arabic word *tawhid* means literally "to make into," "to unify," "to conclude that something is one," "to consider as one," "to declare that God is one," and "to believe in God's Unity." In other words, God is One; His Essence and Attributes are unique; there is no cause for His Acts, nor does He possess any partner in them; and since He is known in this way by those who possess faith and certainty, their knowledge of this Unity is called *tawhid* or "the profession of Unity." In God's own words, "Your God is One God" *(Koran,* II: 163).

Specialists in the *Shari'at* hold that *tawhid* is the verbal acknowledgement of divine Unity, as well as the heartfelt belief that God is, indeed, One.

TAWHID ACCORDING TO THE SUFIS

What is this tawhid, *this learning God's Unity?*
Burning oneself to ashes before the One!
But when my pen attempts to describe this state
The pen is shattered and the paper torn to shreds.

Rumi

Tawhid is to see and know nothing but God. To consider oneself as oneself, as a separate entity, is to see God as two. To not know oneself is to see the Act of God, not one's own actions. What most people call *tawhid* is not *tawhid* at all. Speech is an attribute of the tongue, faith an attribute of the innermost consciousness; on the basis of these two, most believers consider themselves to have professed *tawhid.* Speech and faith, however, are attributes of created beings, not of God in His Oneness—and he who perceives multiple attributes cannot truly be said to have professed Unity.

He who has genuine *tawhid* is conscious of nothing but God; if he remains aware of his own inmost consciousness, obviously he is conscious of something other than God. Thus, he has not truly realized the station of *tawhid.* The heart possessed of *tawhid* is God's own sanctuary, and God allows no other but Himself within His shrine. When *tawhid* gains strength within the Sufi's innermost consciousness, neither heaven nor earth impinge upon that consciousness. (Adapted from the *Rasā'el* of Shāh Nimatullah Vali)

THE PILLARS OF *TAWHID*

Tawhid has seven pillars:

1. He who professes *tawhid* must distinguish between eternality and temporality; that is, he must know that with respect to the Essence, Attributes, and Acts, the Eternal is unlike the temporal.

2. He must know that the temporal cannot attain the Eternal.

3. He must not consider God's Attributes equal to those of created beings.

4. He must not confuse causality with the Station of Lordship.

5. He must know that God is too great to be affected or His view altered by the power of the temporal. In other words, His pleasure is not earned by obedience nor His

anger by disobedience. Service is not rewarded by proximity, nor does infidelity lead to distance. If the opposite were true, the Eternal would have to be considered as mutable—which would be absurd.

6. He must know that God is free of differentiation and deliberation. Differentiation characterizes the soul in need, which must distinguish between good and evil in order to gain profit and avoid loss. But since God is in need of nothing, it is impossible for Him to differentiate in this way. As for deliberation, this is an act performed when something is hidden, in order to be able to judge its goodness or evilness. Yet nothing is hidden from God, so there can be no deliberation for Him.

7. He must know that one cannot come to know God by analogy, by comparing Him with anything. (Adapted from the *Sharh-e ta'arrof*)

THE PRINCIPLES OF *TAWHID*

Abol-Hasan Hosri has described the principles of *tawhid* in the following way:

> There are five principles of *tawhid:* elimination of temporality; affirmation of the Eternal; migration from one's homeland; separation from brothers; and forgetting what one knows and does not know.
> The elimination of temporality means the denial of any connection between temporal things and *tawhid,* the recognition of the impossibility of temporal events transpiring within His Holy Essence.
> Affirming the Eternal means believing that God always is.

Migrating from one's homeland means that the seeker must cut himself off from all with which the ego *(nafs)* is familiar, all in which the heart finds satisfaction, in which the natural disposition takes its repose. That is, he must migrate from worldly custom. . . .

Separation from brothers means turning away from companionship with anything other than God. . . .

Forgetting what one knows and does not know about *tawhid* means that whatever men have said and theorized about *tawhid* is rejected by *tawhid* itself. . . . All personal initiative must be negated if true knowledge of *tawhid* is to be attained—and both knowledge and ignorance depend on personal initiative, the one based on insight, the other on forgetfulness. *(Sharh-e ta'arrof)*

TAWHID, ETTEHĀD AND VAHDAT: DEFINITIONS AND DISTINCTIONS

Whereas *tawhid* means "to make one," *ettehād* (unification) means "to become one." This distinction clarifies the fact that *tawhid,* at least from a linguistic point of view, contains a blemish, an affectation of selfhood. Hence, when the Sufi becomes firmly rooted in Absolute Oneness and loses all perception of duality, he is said to have reached unification or *ettehād.* Certain near-sighted people have imagined that this means the servant becomes united with God. But this is not so. (How exalted is God above such a thing!) Rather, in unification, the Sufi sees all as God, without affection, and declares, "If everything 'other-than-He' is He, then all is One!"

The Sufi who sees by the light of divine theophany

perceives nothing but God: seer, sight, and seen vanish without trace; being itself disappears. Thus does he exclaim:

I am He whom I love,
He whom I love is I!

Hallāj

To the one in such a station, it becomes clear that when Hallāj said, "I am the Truth!" or Bayāzid, "Glory be to me! How exalted is my station!", they were making no crude claim to divinity but rather expressing the negation of their own separate existence.

Vahdat, or "Oneness," is above even unification. To speak of "unification," after all, still involves a faint trace of multiplicity which is missing from "Oneness." In Oneness, all disappears: both stillness and motion; meditation and remembrance; wayfaring and the Path; seeking, seeker, and saying. "When speech reaches God, stop!" *(Rasa'el, Shah Nimatullah Vali)*

TAWHID AND INVOCATION

Different Sufi masters have made use of various invocations in the realization of *tawhid.* For example:

1. *Lā elāha ellallāh* ("No god but God"). This invocation is for ordinary believers. It denies the divinity of anything other than God. Most authorities consider it an expression of absolute *tawhid.*

2. *Lā howa ellā hu* ("No he but He"). Mohammad Ghazzali was of the opinion that this invocation was still closer to the meaning of *tawhid,* since it negates all he-ness, she-

ness, and it-ness in the face of God's ipseity—for all he-nesses derive from His He-ness. [In Arabic, the third person singular pronoun *hu* signifies he, she, and it.]

3. *Lā anta ellā anta* ("No thou but thou"). Kattāni considered this invocation still more perfect, since the pronoun *hu* refers to an absent thing or person. Those who use this invocation negate the thou-ness of those who see themselves in the station of thou-ness, alluding to presence rather than absence.

4. *Lā anā ellā anā* ("No I but I"). This invocation was advocated by Bāyazid. Devotees of this expression hold that the use of "Thou" still suggests a separation of subject and object, whereas such duality is impossible in the realm of Oneness.

5. Finally, some of those who profess Unity find that duality, individual existence, and he-ness alike all represent illusory points of view, artificially grafted, as it were, onto the Self-subsistent Essence. Thus, they drown all three terms in the sea of obliteration.

THE LEVELS OF *TAWHID*

Certain masters have considered *tawhid* to contain different levels. A number of these masters have spoken of a *tawhid* of the common believers, of the elect, and of the elect of the elect.

1. Tawhid of the Common Believers

Ruzbehān has written of this level of *tawhid:*

The *tawhid* of the common believer consists of

77

travelling within the signs of God after having been guided by Him and of seeking God by means of the intellect, the light of faith, and the witnessing of temporal things, until relief is found from the turmoil of doubt and confusion and one ends in the affirmation of God's Oneness. Thus delivered from all thoughts originating from the ego *(nafs)*, the believer discovers the glorification of His Eternal Essence and the total non-existence of anything analogous to His Attributes of Might. He comes to realize that God is One in every respect, that His Essence is One in His Attributes, and vice-versa. He separates His Eternality from all temporality, His Majestic Being from all created things. Rejecting all vain fantasy from his heart, he realizes God's dissimilarity to everything that enters the imagination and understanding. *(Resālat al-Qods)*

Of this same level of *tawhid,* Dhon-Nun has said:

One must understand that God has power over things but is not *involved* in them; He makes things but does not manipulate them; the cause of all things is His making, but His making has no cause; in heaven above and on earth below, there is none that governs but God. Whatever your imagination can grasp, He is other than that. *(al-Loma')*

On the same subject, Jonayd has declared:

This level of *tawhid* involves the isolation of the Object of *tawhid* by actualizing (within oneself) the all-embracing Oneness in the perfection of Absolute Unity—for He is 'the One, who begets not, nor was He begotten.' *(Koran,* CXII: 3) This process of isolation is carried out by negating all opposites,

78

equals, likenesses, and all things worshipped other
than God, without falling into the errors of
comparing Him to anything, characterizing Him by
false Attributes, representing Him in any form, or
explaining Him through analogy. He is God, the
One, the Eternal Refuge, the Unique. 'Nothing is
like Him, and He is the All-hearing, the All-seeing.'
(Koran, XLII: 11) *(Ibid)*

2. Tawhid of the Elect

Jonayd has defined this level of *tawhid* as "the servant's hurling of himself into the current of Divine predestination; over him then flow the properties of God's
Power in the ocean depths of *tawhid.*" He goes on to say:

> This station is achieved through the annihilation
> of himself, of the creatures' attraction of him toward
> themselves, and of his response to the realities of his
> own existence and oneness. It takes place within the
> reality of proximity to Him. All sense and movement
> cease for the servant here, for God has allowed him
> within the very thing that God demands from him:
> that his end return to its beginning, that he be now
> as he was before he was. *(Resālat al-Qoshayri)*

Shebli, when asked about this level of *tawhid,* replied:

> Woe to you! Whoever answers such a question
> in words is a heretic; whoever makes allusions to
> God is a dualist; whoever remains silent is an
> ignoramus. If you imagine you have reached Union,
> you have lost it all; if you point to Him, you are but
> an idol-worshipper, if you speak of Him, you are
> unmindful; if you think yourself near, you are far; if
> you pretend to love Him, you are lost. Whatever

your fancy or reason can discern about Him, however perfect and subtle, merely reflects back upon yourself, being created and timebound like yourself. *(al-Loma')*

Ruzbehan has defined the *tawhid* of the elect in the following way:

The *tawhid* of the Elect is that they behold all of created existence wiped out before God's Tremendousness. They find all beings nonexistent in God's Lordship, in the overwhelming face of Eternity's light. God existed in Eternity before anything came into being: the elect see that nothing has changed, that nothing exists not drowned in His Command. This realization is attained through contemplation based on right doctrine *('elm),* for doctrine belongs to all believers, but contemplation only to the Elect. Created existence is seen as a mere polo-ball, knocked about by the mallet of Divine Power on the polo-field of God, from beginninglessness to endlessness and back again.

The *tawhid* of the common believer is to progress to God from the world of the Visible, of Dominion, which in its outward form is the Macrocosm. The *tawhid* of the elect is to progress to God from oneself, for in form man is the World of Meaning and the Mansion of Theophany, the Greatest Sign—despite the fact that compared to the Universe he is so tiny.

The difference between the two types of *tawhid* lies in this: the common believer is hamstrung by questions of proof and problems of intellect, while the elect, in their knowledge of God, are annihilated from all micro- and macrocosmic evidence. They find annihilation in the divine Subsistence and are forever naughted in the divine Being; His eternal Properties govern them, and they are ruled by submission. *(Resālat al-Qods)*

Finally, Ansari has written:

The *tawhid* of the elect is established through the realities; it results from denying outward causes, from transcending the chatter of the intellect and all attachment to 'evidence.' One must contemplate no signpost to *tawhid,* no cause for trust, and no way to deliverance; one contemplates only God's pre-eminence in Decision and Knowledge, His ordering of things, putting right things in right places at right times and concealing them in outward forms and appearances. One must gain a sound knowledge of one's own shortcomings and set out on the path of nullifying temporality. This is the *tawhid* of the elect, established through the science of annihilation and purified through the science of All-comprehensive-ness, which attracts seekers to those who occupy these stations. *(Manāzel as-sā'erin)*

3. Tawhid of the Elect of the Elect

According to Ruzbehan:

The *tawhid* of the elect of the elect is this: that they journey from God to God. This journey is made when man's holy spirit dismounts from all the various steeds of temporality—disposing of all direction, place, progress, and time, and driving the asses of vain fantasy from the stable of the stallion of light. Such a person anoints the eyes of understanding and comprehension with the collyrium of non-attainment. He renders inactive the

machinations of sense and unreasoning
consciousness and cuts off the officious tongue of the
intellect with the scissors of dissimilarity (i.e., the
profession that God is not 'like' anything else). In
the bazaar of jealous *tawhid,* he cuts off the smug
head of the ego *(nafs).* With love's blows, he routs
the army of self-will and passion, the army of Satan.
He does not leave God's city, the heart, without the
bustling activity of servanthood. With the storm of
nothingness and the axe of existence, he demolishes
the house of natural dispositions, crowded with
human frailties. He rolls up like scrolls both
microcosm and macrocosm with all their evidence
and proofs, then hurls them into the hiding-place of
non-existence that he might walk a few steps in
Eternity unhampered by the burdens of time. Free at
last of the tumultuous hordes of creation, he dives
into the ocean of nothingness that he might be
annihilated from himself, then up bobs his head in
the sea of Divine Subsistence. Without self, he sees
God through God, and in the sky of Ipseity he flies
with the wings of Lordship in the strength of his
servanthood.

The reality of *tawhid* cannot be reduced to
speech—for if it could be, this would be unbelief.
Whoever professes Unity, his attributes cannot be
described—for here to speak is but ignorance.
(Resālat al-qods)

Ansari has described this final stage as "a *tawhid* that
God has singled out for Himself, considering it worthy of
His measure." He explains:

To the inmost consciousness of a group of His
favorites, He displays a flash of it, striking them
mute in terms of its description and rendering them

82

unable to convey it to others. Those who hint can only allude to 'the nullification of time and affirmation of Eternity,' although even this m[is] misleading and must itself be nullified in turn.

This *tawhid* has been alluded to by the masters of the Path. They have woven fine phrases about it and written little essays on it, but verbosity only buries it deeper, descriptions only drive it away, and expositions only increase its complexity.

Ascetics and Sufis alike have pointed to this *tawhid;* the People of Reverence have aimed at it, and those who speak of the 'Reality of All-Comprehensiveness' have had it in mind. But in it, all allusions are extirpated; no tongue speaks of it, and no expressions do justice to it—for *tawhid* lies beyond that which created things can grasp, or time englobe, or causes and reasons express. *(Manāzel as-sā'erin)*

Finally, in regard to this three part division, Abu Hafs has said:

> The *tawhid* of the common believers is to become disgusted with 'other-than-God' through discernment. The *tawhid* of the elect is to arrive at the One. The *tawhid* of the elect of the elect is to arrive at the One without going through 'union.' "
> *(Tabaqāt as-sufiyah)*

*   *   *

In regard to the levels of *tawhid,* Shah Nimatullah has written:

> Of those who profess Unity, some have said that it is at first a science, then a spiritual state, then again a science. The first science is but a pointer, an

indication; it is the science of the common believers, those well-versed in exoteric knowledge who seek the solar brilliance of the theophanies of the Most Holy Essence and the lights of the effusions of the Holy Attributes, using in their search both the intellect's radiant lamp and the glowing rays of candles handled down by tradition.[1]

The intellect is their companion and guide through the realm of transmitted signs; they seek to explain the Actor through His Acts, the Creator through his creation. Accidental knowledge allows them to perceive the rose by its color and musk by its scent, as if they were to say, "I hear the mill-wheel creak, but see no grinding!"

In the *tawhid* that is based upon a spiritual state, he who professes Unity becomes imbued with divine characteristics and is qualified by beginningless and endless Attributes. As the Prophet has said, "Take on God's traits!" In other words, become qualified by the divine Attributes. God, not himself, governs all his actions. As God told the Prophet, "Thou didst not throw when thou threwest, but God threw." *(Koran,* VIII: 17)

The second science of *tawhid* is that of contemplation in respect to Oneness. That is, in this station he contemplates only the One who has manifested Himself through the theophany of the many 'ones,' as the world is made up of units which

1. This is a reference to the customary two-part division of the sciences in Islam into the 'intellectual' sciences, or those that can be derived with the unaided human intelliegence—such as mathematics and astronomy, and the 'transmitted' sciences, or those that must be handed down—such as grammar, *Koranic* interpretation, hadith.

have come to be called 'compound things' because they are related to one another. *(Rasā'el, Shāh Nimatullah Vali)*

*   *   *

Ezzad-Din Kāshāni has defined the levels of *tawhid* in the following way:

> The first level of *tawhid* is that realized by faith, the second by science, the third by spritual state, and the fourth only by God.

> 1. The *tawhid* realized by faith occurs when the servant assents in his heart and attests with his tongue to the uniqueness of the description of the Divinity and to the fact that God alone is worthy of worship, according to the indications of the verses of the Holy *Koran* and the *hadith* of the Prophet. This kind of *tawhid* is the result of giving credence to him who has brought the Tidings and of believing the truthfulness of those Tidings. Such a *tawhid* is acquired from the outward aspect of science. Holding fast to it is profitable since it frees one from open idolatry and brings one into the ranks of Islam. Since it is necessary for the Sufis to have faith, they share in this kind of *tawhid* with the common believers. However, the Sufis alone possess the other levels.

> 2. The *tawhid* realized by science is derived from the inward aspect of science, which is called the 'science of certainty.' In this case, at the beginning of the Path of Sufism, the servant knows with certainty that the True Existent and the Absolute Producer of Effects is none other than the Lord of the World, and he considers all essences, attributes, and acts to

be effaced and annihilated in His Essence, Attributes, and Acts. He knows every essence to be a spark of light from the Absolute Essence and every attribute to be one of the rays of the light of the Absolute Attributes. Thus, wherever he finds a science, a power, a will, a hearing, or a seeing, he considers it to be one of the effects of the Science, Power, Will, Hearing, or Seeing of God. This holds true in the case of all attributes and acts. This level is one of the first levels of the *tawhid* that pertains to the elite and the Sufis, but its beginning is grafted upon the stem of the *tawhid* of the common believers.

Similar to this level is a level which the shortsighted call by the same name but which is not the same. Rather, it is merely a formal *tawhid,* devoid of any value. This is the *tawhid* of a clever and astute person who, as a result of study or listening to others, conceives of the meaning of *tawhid,* thereby inscribing an impression of its science in his mind. Such an individual, during discussions and arguments, will make empty remarks about the subject, indicating that the (spiritual) state of *tawhid* has not had the slightest effect upon him.

Although the *tawhid* realized by science is below the level of that realized by (spiritual) states, it nevertheless does carry a mixture of the latter along with it. The *Koranic* verse, 'And its mixture is *Tasnim,* the fountain at which drink those brought nigh' *(Koran,* LXXXIII: 27), is the description of the wine of this *tawhid.* Therefore, he who reaches this state spends most of his time in joy and delight. Through the effect of this mixture, which derives from the realization of (spiritual) states, part of the darkness of his formal limitations is eliminated. Thus, in certain activities, he acts according to his science and does not see the existence of intermediate causes, which are the links of the Divine Acts, interposing themselves. But in most of his states and hours, he remains veiled from the requirements of his science because of the remnants of the darkness of existence. Through this kind of *tawhid,* part of his hidden idolatry is removed.

3. The *tawhid* realized by (spiritual) states exists when the state of *tawhid* becomes the inherent description of the essence of the one who professes it and when all of the darkness of the formal limitations of one's existence, but for a slight remainder, become annihilated and vanish because of the sway of *tawhid's* radiant light: The light of the science of *tawhid* becomes concealed and contained within the light of such a person's (spiritual) state, like the light of the stars within the light of the sun. When the morning becomes clear, its brightness shines forth and embraces the brightness of the light of the stars.

In this station, through the contemplation of the beauty of the One, the existence of the one who professes Unity becomes so absorbed by the Reality of All-comprehensiveness that he sees nothing but the One's Essence and Attributes. This is true to such an extent that he sees this very *tawhid* to be the Attribute of the One, not of himself, and even this seeing he sees to be His Attribute. In this way, like a drop of water, his existence falls under the dominion of the tumultuous waves of the sea of *tawhid,* and he is drowned in All-Comprehensiveness. This is why Jonayd said, *"Tawhid* is a supra-formal state in which formal limitations disappear, all knowledge is contained, and God is as He was from all Eternity." In a similar manner, Ibn Atā' has said, *"Tawhid* is to forget *tawhid* in the contemplation of the Majesty of the One, until you subsist through the One, not through *tawhid.*"

The source of this *tawhid* is the light of contemplation *(moshāhadah),* while the source of the *tawhid* realized by science is the light of meditation *(morāqabah).* Through this *tawhid,* the great majority of the formal limitations of the human disappear, just as most of the darkness of the earth is dispelled by the sway of the manifestation of the sun's light. Through the *tawhid* realized by science though, only some of these formal limitations disappear, like the darkness that is dispelled by the appearance of the light of the moon with most of the darkness remaining. The reason that some formal limitations still remain in the *tawhid* realized by (spiritual) states is that the one who has realized this state would otherwise not be able to keep his acts in good order and his words in strict discipline. Hence, the *tawhid* that is truly worthy cannot be achieved in this life. This is why Abū Ali Daqqāq has said, "Tawhid is a creditor whose debt cannot be paid, and a guest whose rights cannot be fulfilled." Nevertheless, through this kind of *tawhid,* most of one's hidden idolatry is removed.

Occasionally, the elite among those who profess Unity catch a glimpse during their lifetime of the reality of unadulterated *tawhid,* in which the effects and formal limitations of existence are annihilated completely as if by a flash of lightning. But at once the flash disappears and the remnants of formal limitations return. In this brief spiritual state, all of the remnants of hidden idolatry are removed. Beyond this level of *tawhid,* no other level is possible for man.

As for the tawhid realized by God Himself, the meaning is that God in all eternity is described and qualified by Oneness and Singularity in His own Self, not through the *tawhid* of others. "God was, and nothing was with Him," and now too He maintains His beginningless qualification of being the One and Unique ("And now He is as He was."), and for all eternity He shall keep this description ("All things are perishing except His Face."). (XXVIII: 88) God did not say, "will perish," for He wanted it to be known that the existence of all things is perishing in His Being *today.* Only those who are still veiled postpone the observance of this until tomorrow. In the case of the Possessors of Spiritual Insight and the Masters of Contemplation, who have attained freedom from the narrow confines of time and space, this promise by God is ready cash. As it says in the *Koran,* "the day that they see as far off, We see as nigh." (LXX: 6) The Might of His Singularity and the Subjugating Power of His Oneness leave no room for the existence of any but Him. This is the true and correct *tawhid,* free from the stain of imperfection. But the *tawhid* realized by the angels and men is imperfect because of the imperfection of existence.

* * *

None has given justice to the tawhid *of the One, for whoever expresses it denies it.*
The tawhid *of one who speaks of it as His qualification is but a loan nullified by the One.*
Only His tawhid *is the true* tawhid; *the description of one who describes Him (as One) is heretical.*

Ansāri

Ansāri has written extensively on the levels of *tawhid*. In the *Sad maydān,* he has defined the levels of *tawhid* in the following manner:

Tawhid is (1) to say one; (2) to see One; and (3) to know One. In His own words, "So know that there is no god but God." *(Koran,* XLVII: 19)

1. 'To say One' is the beginning of all science, the gate of all knowledge of the world and of religion, and the dividing line between friend and foe. The testimony of faith ("There is no god but God") is science; its foundation is sincerity, and its precondition is fidelity.

The outward and inward nature of the formula of this *tawhid* can be described in three different ways. First, as a bearing of witness to God's Oneness in Essence, and His purity from any associate, spouse, child, partner or assistant. Second, as a bearing of witness to God's Oneness in Attributes. In them he has no likeness. He possesses Attributes imperceptible by the intellect, attributes whose natures are impossible to understand, comprehend, or imagine. The names of these attributes have nothing in common with them and are not similar to them. Third, as a bearing of witness to God's Oneness in His true and beginningless Names— Names which are for Him a reality, even though for all others they are but borrowed labels. Though His creations do, of course, possess names, His names are Real, Eternal, without origin, and worthy of Him, while the names of created things are, after all, created and temporal in keeping with their nature. Those of His Names that are uniquely His, and that describe nothing other than Him, are Allah and Rahmān ('the Merciful').

2. 'To see Him as One' depends upon destinies, lots and bounties. That is, Oneness in destinies means that He is alone in the determination of fate, One in His beginningless, all-embracing Science and Wisdom, which no one but He possesses. To realize this truth a man must be wise; to consider it as correct he must be bewildered, and to continue with it he must be strong. No one possesses this power of fate but God.

Oneness in lots means that He Himself bestows portions among His creatures, each in accordance with the destiny and best interest of that creature, and at the appropriate time.

As for Oneness in bounties, this is through His Unity. He is the Bestower and the One. No one else deserves gratitude and thanks; no one else possesses strength and might or the power to grant or withhold bounty.

3. 'To know One' refers to service, conduct, and resolution. In service, it means to forego leadership, observe sincerity, and control thought. In conduct, it means to purify the inmost consciousness, actualize remembrance, and cling steadily to confidence. In resolution, it means to lose and to forget everything but God, and to be delivered, through the heart's freedom, from all other than He. *(Sad maydān)*

In the *Tabaqāt as-sufiyyah,* Ansāri has defined the levels of *tawhid* as follows:

Tawhid has five levels: (1) the science of *tawhid,* (2) the eye of *tawhid,* (3) the existence of *tawhid,* (4) annihilation in *tawhid,* and (5) the containment of *tawhid* in *tawhid.*

The science of *tawhid* is revealed to the one who

91

professes it through the guidance of his primordial nature, which is in turn approached by theoretical knowledge. This is the highest degree that can be reached by those who limit themselves to transmitted knowledge.

The eye of *tawhid* is approached by the utmost effort of intuitive contemplation. Within it, direct examination through unveiling becomes established, while dispersive and merely evidential modes of perception are suppressed.

The existence of *tawhid* begins when these lesser modes of perception are left behind and one enters into sheer and beginningless Witnessing.

Annihilation in *tawhid* is to transcend mere verbal allusion and to realize the reality of God.

As for the containment of *tawhid* within *tawhid,* it is the drowning of what never was in that which always is.

*   *   *

Finally, according to Hojviri, there are three kinds of *tawhid:*

1. God's *tawhid* of God—that is, His knowledge *('elm)* of His Own Oneness; 2. God's *tawhid* of the creatures—that is, His decision to bestow *tawhid* on the servant and His creation of it within the servant's heart; and 3. the servant's *tawhid* of God—that is, his knowledge *('elm)* of God's Oneness.

WORDS OF THE MASTERS ON *TAWHID*

Abol-'Abbas Sayyāri: *"Tawhid* is that nothing crosses your heart but God." *(Kashf al-mahjub)*

Ebn Khafif: *"Tawhid* is to turn away from the natural

92

constitution, which is by its very nature blind to God's blessings and veiled to His Bounties. One cannot begin to turn toward God until one has turned away from the natural constitution." *(Kashf al-mahjub)*

"When Hallāj was asked to define *tawhid*, he answered that it was to isolate the Eternal from the temporal. Ansāri commented, 'Do you know wherein consists the *tawhid* of the Sufi? Negation of the temporal and affirmation of the Beginningless.' " *(Tabaqāt as-sufiyyah)*

Abu Ya'qub Susi: "Whoever speaks of *tawhid* out of affectation is an idolater. Then what is it? No talk, no discussion, no equal, no likeness, no designation, no state. Only this: 'He was always and always will be.' The measure of *tawhid* is beyond the intellect; its reality is safe from the imagination." *(Tabaqāt as-sufiyah)*

Ansāri: "There are five sciences of the realities: the science of allusion, of reality, of love, of knowledge, and of *tawhid*. This last science is God and nothing but God. The rest is nonsense. 'Other-than-He' is nothing and nobody.

"There also exists the science of *tawhid*, the eye of *tawhid*, the all-comprehensiveness of *tawhid*, and the existence of *tawhid*. But all *tawhid* is useless save *tawhid* itself and the truth of *tawhid*. The completion of *tawhid* without *tawhid* is the denial of *tawhid*.

"The people of allusion are intimate with their own kind; the people of reality leave life aside; the people of love war with their own souls; the people of knowledge go hand-in-hand with Union; but the people of *tawhid* are lost to themselves from themselves in themselves." *(Tabaqāt as-sufiyyah)*

Abu Sa'id: "Once, in the city of Amol, Abol-Abbās Qassāb told me about the time someone asked him to comment on the verse, 'Say: He is God, the One.' *(Koran, CXII: 1).* He replied, ' "Say" is occupation; "He" is allusion; "God" is expression. But the meaning of *tawhid* is beyond all allusion and expression.' " *(Asrār al-tawhid)*

"Abu 'Abdollah Mohammad ebn 'Ali (known as Dāstāni) has said, 'Tawhid coming from you is existent, but in tawhid you are isolated and lost.' In other words, tawhid from you is correct, but you are incorrect in tawhid—for then you are not acting in accordance with God's due. Even the lowest degree of tawhid negates your self-activity in the world and affirms your submission to God in your affairs." (Kashf al-mahjub)

Yusef ebn Hosayn (reported by Abu Sa'id): "He who falls into the sea of tawhid grows thirstier day by day and can never drink his fill—for his thirst is quenched by God alone." (Asrār al-tawhid)

"Ebn 'Atā' said that the sign of authentic tawhid is the forgetting of tawhid, and the true tawhid is that he who professes it is one. That is to say, in his tawhid the servant forgets the vision of tawhid, which is submerged in the vision of God's establishing him in tawhid even before his creation. If God did not desire tawhid for us, we would not want it and would never profess His Unity." (al-Loma')

Shebli: "He has missed the perfume of tawhid who conceptualizes it, witnesses realities, affirms Names, ascribes Attributes, and juggles with descriptions. He who affirms and denies all of these may have the properties and titles of one who professes Unity, but not his reality and existence." (Ibid)

Jāmi: "Tawhid is to make the heart one, that is, to purify it and disengage it from attachment to anything other than God, both in terms of aspiration and desire and in terms of theory and knowledge. In other words, the Sufi's aspiration and desire are cut off from all objects; and all objects of knowlege, all intelligible things, are removed from the eye of his insight. He turns his attention away from every other direction, so that his consciousness and awareness remain fixed upon none but God." (Lavā'eh)

Darvish Mohammad Tabasi: "Tawhid is that one is annihilated in devotion to God and removed from all self-will, and that one habituates the tongue to truth and re-strains the heart from all relationships with 'other than God,' considering it as obliterated." *(Āthār)*

Rovaym: *"Tawhid* is the obliteration of the traces of human nature and the naked presence of the Divinity." *(al-Loma')*

Jonayd: *"Tawhid* is to take leave of the constrictions of formal limitations and to arrive at the spaciousness of annihilation in Eternity." *(Ibid)*

Shebli once asked someone, "Do you know why your *tawhid* is incorrect?" The person answered, "No." Shebli said, "Because you seek Him with 'unto thee.' "[1] *(al-Loma')*

"Shebli once asked someone, 'Do you profess the *tawhid* of human nature or that of Divine Nature?' The man asked, 'Is there a difference?' 'Indeed, yes,' Shebli replied. 'The *tawhid* of human nature is the fear of punishment, but the *tawhid* of the divine Nature is the *tawhid* of glorification.' " *(Ibid)*

Abu Sa'id Kharrāz: "The first station of one who attains and actualizes the science of *tawhid* is the freeing of his heart from thinking-about-things, that he might stand alone with God." *(Ibid)*

Shebli: "The end of *tawhid* is to forget other than *tawhid* through *tawhid.*" *(Ibid)*

Shebli: "Oneness is the subsistence of God through the annihilation of everything other than He." *(Ibid)*

Shebli: "There is no creature in *tawhid;* no one finds God but God. *Tawhid* is God's alone; creatures are but uninvited guests." *(al-Loma')*

Shebli: " 'In *tawhid,* the servant does not attain self-

---

1. As in the *fātihah* of the *Koran* which says, "Unto Thee we seek refuge." Shebli is implying here that the duality inherent in such an attitude precludes the attainment of true *tawhid.* (ed.)

realization until he dreads his own innermost consciousness because of God's manifestation to him.' In other
words, when God overcomes the servant's consciousness,
he reaches a state in which he is unaware of his own 'moment'; if he still retains some awareness of it, one cannot
say that his consciousness has been taken over by God.
Thus, his dread of his own innermost consciousness is as if
he were to say to himself, 'If my *tawhid* were complete I
would have no news of other than God.' That is, he is still
in touch with his own consciousness, the attributes of
which are other than God. Such a one has not truly realized *tawhid.*" *(Sharh-e ta'arrof)*

"Abu Bakr Mohammad ebn Musā Vaseti claimed,
'Whatever can be uttered by the tongue or alluded to and
explained—such as the glorification of God, the detachment from 'other-than-God,' or becoming isolated with
God—all this is caused by something else, and the reality of
tawhid is beyond it.' In other words, what people express
and describe are in fact their own attitudes, temporal in
nature, effects rather than causes, just like themselves.
God's reality is His own description of Himself." *(Ibid)*

"One of the Sufis said, '*Tawhid* is to make yourself
single in *tawhid;* in effect, it is that God not show you to
yourself.' Thus, *tawhid* is 'to know One,' to see none other
than He. If you see something 'other' than Him, that is not
tawhid. In *tawhid,* you must become single in the sense that
you see none but Him, are alone, one for Him, not for
other than He; you see not yourself or your own actions
and know that the Eternal Will and Knowledge have made
you a knower so that you experience God's favor." *(Ibid)*

"One of the Sufis said, 'He who professes Unity is the
one whom God has separated from this world and the next
and all they contain, in order to preserve the exclusiveness
of His Sanctuary.' That is, when the servant finds *tawhid,*
no desire remains in him either for the things of this world
or the world to come, for heaven and earth and 'other-

than-God.' To be busy with such matters is to miss the freedom from care of preoccupation with God. Having reached God, however, he desires nothing but God. That heart which truly attains *tawhid* is God's own Sanctuary. God allows no one entry there. Thus, if anything other than God enters the servant's innermost consciousness, it is a sign that this consciousness is not God's Sanctuary." *(Ibid)*

"Fāres said, '*Tawhid* is not perfected as long as something of detachment from the world remains attached to you.' What he meant by this is that the servant truly becomes one who professes Unity only when he is free of all bonds; if he is attached to anything in the two worlds [even to non-attachment], his *tawhid* is not complete." *(Ibid)*

"Fāres also said, 'He who professes Unity in speech is not "one for Him" in his innermost consciousness.' That is, if he can express *tawhid* in words, it must mean that he can observe his own *tawhid* in order to describe it, and therefore cannot be 'one for God.' If he were observing God, he would have no news of his own *tawhid!*" *(Ibid)*

"Fāres also said, '*Tawhid* is to emerge totally from your own existence, always on the condition that you fulfill your obligations to God, and that nothing occupy you that might drive you from Him.' By 'emerging totally from self,' Fāres meant that you see no attribute or act as your own. You perceive all motion as emanating from His motive Power, all stillness given by His stillness. You see existence through His bestowal of existence and subsistence through His bestowal of subsistence. When you have taken full leave of yourself, you spend generously your spirit and soul in His work, carrying out your duty, but knowing your own inadequacy, not imagining any action as originating with yourself. To love something other than God is to cut yourself off from His Love, and likewise with fear and hope and again with confidence and intimacy. And to desire anything but God, to look at anything else, is to turn

97

your face from Him and to be cut off from the vision of the Divine." *(Ibid)*

This *faqir* (the author) says, "Those who were drowned in the ocean of *tawhid* had no existence that they might speak. What the Sufi masters have said of *tawhid* is not truly its reality; rather, each of them has described his own states, stations, and perceptions. Words and allusions make no way to *tawhid*—and no one knows it but God.

Translated by William Chittick and Peter Wilson.

APPENDIX

What follows below is a compendium of the persons and books mentioned in the text. It should be noted that very little information is provided about certain figures since they are practically unknown with the exception of one or two quotations from them in classical texts. For reference purposes, at least one source (either English or Persian) has usually been provided for each person mentioned. The following abbreviations have been employed:

KM. *The Kashf al-mahjub. The Oldest Persian Treatise on Sufism,* by al-Hujwiri, translated by R.A. Nicholson, London, 1911, reprinted 1970.

MP. *Masters of the Path: A History of the Masters of the Nimatullahi Sufi Order,* by Dr. Javad Nurbakhsh, New York, 1980.

MSM. *Muslim Saints and Mystics. Episodes from the Tadhkirat al-awliyā,* translated by A. J. Arberry, Chicago, 1966.

NF. *Nafahāt al-ons* by Jāmi, ed. by M. Tawhidipur, Tehran, 1336/1957.

TA. *Tadhkerat al-awliyā* by 'Attār, ed. by M. Este'lāmi, Tehran, 1346/1967.

TS. *Tabaqāt as-sufiyah* by Ansāri, ed. by 'A. Habibi, Kabol, 1341/1962.

Abol-'Abbās Nahāvandi: A master of the fourth/tenth century, successor of Ja'far Kholdi. According to some sources he died in 320 A.H./932 A.D.

Abol-'Abbās Qassāb: A master who flourished in the sec-

101

ond half of the fourth/tenth century and was a companion of Abol-Hasan Kharaqāni. KM 161.

Abol-'Abbās Sayyāri: The founder of one of the twelve Sufi orders listed by Hojviri (KM 130); he lived in the third/ninth century. KM 157.

Abol-Fath Bosti (d. 400 A.H./1009-10): A poet who wrote mostly in Arabic and is not known for any special connection to Sufism.

Abol-Hasan Bushanji (d. 348/959): A well-known Sufi master who was a companion of Ebn 'Atā' and spent much of his life in Nayshāpur. TA 521.

Abol-Hasan (or Abol-Hosayn) Hosri (d. 371/981-2): A disciple of Shebli, he lived in Baghdad. KM 160.

Abol-Hasan Kharaqāni (d. 425/1034): One of the great masters, his fame is partly the result of Rumi's anecdotes about him (see especially *Mathnawi,* IV 1802 ff; VI 2044 ff). KM 163.

Abol-Hasan Mozayyen (d. 328/939-40): A companion of Sahl and Jonayd. TS 333.

Abol-Hasan Qannād: A companion of Hallāj. TS 534.

Abol-Hosayn Nuri (d. 295/908): One of the more famous of the early masters. KM 130, MSM 221.

Abol-Hosayn Sirvāni, the younger: A disciple of Sirvāni the elder, he was a companion of such masters as Jonayd and Shebli. TS 482.

Abol-Hosayn Zanjāni (third/ninth century): TS 560.

Abol-Qāsem Jonayd (d. 298/910): One of the most famous of the Sufi masters and the head of the "Baghdad School." KM 128, MP 20, MSM 199.

Abot-Tib Sāmeri: TS 560.

Abu 'Abdollāh 'Abdol-Vāhed ebn Zayd (d. 177/793): A companion of Hasan Basri. TS 111.

Abu 'Abdollāh Ahmad ebn Mohammad al-Jalā' (d. 306/918-19): A companion of Jonayd. KM 134.

Abu 'Abdollāh ebn Khafif (d. 371/981-2): A famous master from Shiraz, he is the author of a number of books. KM 158, MSM 257.

Abu 'Abdollāh Mohammad ebn 'Ali, known as Dāstāni (fourth/tenth century): KM 164.

Abu 'Abdollāh Mohammad ebn Fadl Balkhi (d. 319/931): A disciple of Ahmad ebn Khadruyah. KM 140.

Abu 'Abdollāh Rudbāri (d. 369/979-80): A cousin of Abu 'Ali Rudbāri, he was a Sufi master in Damascus. TS 470.

Abu 'Ali Daqqāq (d. 405/1014-15 or 412/1021-2): This famous master was a disciple of Nasrābādi and was learned in many sciences. KM 162.

Abu 'Ali Rudbāri (d. 322 or 323/943-5): One of the great masters and companion of Jonayd, Nuri, and Ebn al-Jalā'. KM 157, MP 23.

Abu 'Amr Demashqi (d. 320/932): A companion of Dhon-Nun and Ebn al-Jalā'. TS 328.

Abu 'Amr Najid (d. 336/947-8): A companion of Jonayd. TA 727.

Abu Bakr Kattāni (d. 322/934): A native of Baghdad and companion of Jonayd. MSM 253.

Abu Bakr Qabbāni: TS 560.

Abu Bakr Vāseti, Mohammad ebn Musā (d. after 320/932): According to Attār, he was the greatest master of his time; one of the earliest disciples of Jonayd. KM 154.

Abu Eshāq ebn Ebrāhim: A contemporary of Abu 'Abdollāh ebn Khafif, he was a master in Kāzerun, near Shiraz. NF 254.

Abu Ghilān Samarqandi: A companion of Jonayd. NF 141.

Abu Hafs Haddād Nayshāburi (d. 265/878-9): A blacksmith who became one of the famous masters of Khorāsān. KM 123, MSM 192.

Abu Mansur Mu'ammer Isfahāni (fourth/tenth century): TS 536.

Abu Mohammad Jorayri (d. 311/923-4): One of Jonayd's greatest disciples. TA 579.

Abu Mohammad Morta'esh (d. 328/939-40): A companion of Abu Hafs and Jonayd. TA 515.

Abu Mohammad Rāsebi (d. 367/977-8): A master in Baghdad, he was a companion of Ebn 'Atā and Jorayri. NF 269.

Abu No'aym Esfahāni (d. 430/1038-9): A Sufi and author of many books, including *Helyat al-awliyā'* (q.v.).

Abu Nasr Sarrāj (d. 378/988): The author of *al-Loma'* (q.v.), he was a disciple of Morta'esh and met many of the great masters, such as Sari and Sahl. TA 639.

Abu 'Othmān Maghrebi (d. 373/983-4): See MP 26, KM 158.

Abu Rayhān Biruni (d. 442/1051): Probably the most famous natural scientist in Islamic history, he is the author of numerous works on astronomy, mathematics, geography, etc., including the well-known *India,* translated in the nineteenth century by Sachau.

Abu Sa'id Abel-Khayr (d. 440/1049): One of the most famous early masters, especially because of his biography, *Asrār at-tawhid* (q.v.). See Nicholson, *Studies in Islamic Mysticism* (Cambridge, 1921, ch.1)

Abu Sa'id 'Arābi (d. 340/951-2): A companion of Jonayd and Nuri. TS 414.

Abu Sa'id Kharrāz (d. 286/899): A companion of Dhon-Nun and Sari, he is said to have been the first to use the terms *fanā'* (annihilation) and *baqā'* (subsistence). KM 143, MSM 218.

Abu Sāleh of Basra: A companion of Sahl. TS 560.

Abu Sawdā: A companion of Hallāj.

Abu Solaymān Dārāni (in some sources, Dārā'i) (d. 205/ 820): One of the famous early masters. KM 112.

Abu Torāb Nakhshabi (d. 245/859): A master from Khorasan. KM 121.

Abu Ya'qub Susi: He was a master of the late third/ninth century. TS 278.

Ahmad Khadruyah (d. 240/854): A prominent citizen of Balkh, he was a companion of Bāyazid. KM 119, MSM 173.

'Ali ebn Bondār Sayrafi (d. 359/970): This famous Sufi from Nayshāpur was a companion of Hosri, Abu 'Othmān Maghrebi, and Abd'Abdollah Khafif. TS 247.

'Ali ebn Sahl Esfahāni (d. 280/893): A companion of Abu Torāb and Jonayd. KM 143.

'Amr ebn 'Othmān Makki (291/904): A disciple of Jonayd. KM 138, MSM 214.

Anas ebn Mālek (d. 93/711-12): A companion of the Prophet and an important transmitter of *Hadith.*

Ansāri, Khwājah 'Abdollāh, known as Shaykh al-Islam and the Pir of Herat (d. 481/1088): A master who wrote such well known works as the *Monājāt* ("Intimate Conversations"—translated into English at least twice), *Tabaqāt as-sufiyah* (q.v.) and *Manāzil as-sā'irin* (q.v.).

Asrār at-tawhid (The Mysteries of Tawhid): A biography of Abu Sa'id Abel-Khayr, written by his great-great-grandson in beautiful and simple Persian.

Athār (The Works): The collected Persian works of Tabasi (q.v.), recently published in Tehran by the Nimatullahi Khaniqah.

'Attār (d. 618/1221): A famous Persian Sufi poet and author of the *Tadhkerat al-awliyā'* (q.v.).

Avāref al-ma'āref (Gifts of Knowledge): A classic textbook of Sufi theory and practice written by Shehāb ed-Din 'Omar Suhravardi (q.v.). See *Mesbah el-hedāyah.*

Bābā Tāher Hamadāni (d. 410/1019-20): A Sufi famous for his poems in a Persian dialect and for his Arabic aphorisms.

Bahā'i (d. 1031/1622): Bahā'od-Din 'Āmeli, known as Shaykh-e Bahā'i, was a famous figure of Safavid Isfahan, a Sufi, doctor of the Shari'at, astronomer, mathematician, architect, and author of over 80 works in many fields.

Bāyazid Bastāmi (d. 261/874 or 264/877): One of the most famous of all Sufis, known especially for his "ecstatic" utterances. KM 106, MSM 100.

Beshr al-Hāfi (d. 227/841-2): Besides being a Sufi, he was an authority on *Hadith.* KM 105.

Bondār ebn al-Hosayn as-Sufi (d. 353): A disciple of Shebli. TS 422.

Dhon-Nun Mesri (d. 246/861): A famous early Sufi from Egypt who is said to have known the occult sciences and the secret of the Egyptian hieroplyphs. MSM 87.

Ebn 'Atā', Abol-'Abbās (d. 309/922): A close companion of Jonayd. MSM 236.

Ebn al-Jalā' (d. 306/918): He met Dhon-Nun and was a companion of Jonayd and Nuri. TA 497.

Ebn Yazdānyār, Hosayn ebn 'Ali (d. 333/944-5): A Sufi master who is often remembered for his outward differences with other masters such as Shebli. TS 390.

'Ezzoddin Kāshāni (d. 735/1334-5): A member of the Suhravardi order, he wrote the *Mesbāh al-hedāyah* and other important works.

Fāres Baghdādi (third/ninth century): A disciple of Hallāj. NF 154.

Ghazzāli (d. 505/1111): A Sufi and theologian who wrote numerous works and is famous for giving Sufism a more respected position among the doctors of the *Shari'at*. Numerous studies of him have been written in European languages.

Hallāj (d. 309/922): The famous martyr and archetypal intoxicated lover of God. KM 150, MSM 264.

Hasan of Basra (d. 110/728): One of the greatest early saints. MP 4, MSM 19.

Helyat al-awliyā' (The Adornment of the Saints): A voluminous Arabic history of the saints written by Abu No'aym Esfahāni.

Hojviri (d. 465/1072-3): The author of *Kashf al-mahjub*.

Ja'far Kholdi (d. 348/960-1): A disciple of Jonayd. KM 156.

Ja'far as-Sādeq (148/765): The sixth Shi'ite Imam, he was the greatest Sufi master of his time.

Jāmi (d. 898/1492): A famous Persian Sufi poet, he was also the author of many prose works in both Arabic and Persian. He had considerable influence in spreading the teachings of Ibn 'Arabi.

Jonayd: See Abol-Qāsem.

Jorayri: See Abu Mohammad.

Kashf al-mahjub (The Unveiling of the Veiled): A classic Persian text on Sufism by Hojviri, translated into English by Nicholson. KM.

Kashkūl (The Dervish Begging Bowl): A voluminous Arabic compendium of Sufi philosophy and literature by Shaykh-e Bahā-i.

Kashshāf estelāhāt al-fonun (The Unveiler of the Terminology of the Arts): A well-known traditional dictionary.

Kharrāz: See Abu Sa'id.

107

Kholāsa-ye sharh-e ta'arrof (The Summary of Sharh-e ta'arrof): An eighth/fourteenth century summary of the *Sharh-e ta'arrof* (q.v.) which drops most of the long anecdotes and explanations.

Lawā'eh (Flashes): A beautiful Persian summary of Ibn 'Arabi's teachings by Jāmi, translated into English by Whinfield.

Al-Loma' (Gleams): One of the earliest Arabic textbooks on Sufi teaching and practice by Abu Nasr Sarrāj. Edited and abstracted by Nicholson *(The Kitab al-Loma',* London, 1914).

Maghrebi (d. 809/1406-7): A well-known Persian Sufi poet and follower of Ibn 'Arabi's school. See also "Abu 'Othman."

Majmu'e-ye āthār-e fārsi: The Collected Persian Works of Shihābad-Din Sohravardi, the illuminationist philosopher.

Mamshād Dinavari (d. 299/911-12): A companion of Jonayd and Nuri. TA 610.

Ma'ruf Karkhi (d. 200/815-6): The master of Sari. KM 113, MP 15, MSM 161.

Mesbāh al-hedāyah (The Lamp of Guidance): A Persian revision of the *Avāref al-ma'āref* (q.v.) by 'Ezzoddin Kāshāni, and a classic Sufi textbook. It was partially translated into English by Wilberforce Clarke as *The 'Awarifu-l-ma'ārif* (Calcutta, 1891; N.Y. 1970).

Mohammad ebn Ahmad al-Moqre' (d. 366/976-7): A companion of Rovaym, Jorayri, and Ebn 'Atā'. TS 476.

Mohammad ebn 'Ali Qassāb (d. 275/888-9): A master of Jonayd. TS 182.

Mohammad ebn Eshāq (d. 150 or 151/767-8): A well-known historian, whose *Life of Muhammad* was translated by Guillaume.